SWU-800- 011

UNIFORMS OF RUSSIAN ARMY DURING THE YEARS 1825-1855 VOL. 11

UNDER THE REIGN OF NICHOLAS I
EMPEROR OF RUSSIA BETWEEN 1825 TO 1855
SERVICE TROOPS, MEDICAL, CIVILIAN & OTHERS

From the Viskovatov's greatest work:
"Historical description of the clothing and
arms of the Russian Army"

SOLDIERSHOP PUBLISHING

AUTHOR

Aleksandr Vasilevich Viskovatov born 22 April (4 May New Style) 1804, died 27 February (11 March) 1858 in St. Petersburg, Russian military historian. He graduated from the 1st Cadet Corps and served in the artillery, the hydrographic depot of the Naval Ministry, and then in the Department of Military Educational Institutions. He mainly studied historical artifacts and the histories of military units. Viskovatov's greatest work was the Historical Description of the Clothing and Arms of the Russian Army.

Title: UNIFORMS OF RUSSIAN ARMY DURING THE YEARS 1825-1855. VOL. 11 -Under the reign of Nicholas I emperor of Russia between 1825-1855
By A.V.Viskovatov. Serie edit by Luca S. Cristini. First edition by Soldiershop. June 2019
Cover & Art Design: Luca S. Cristini. Plates re-colorations by Anna Cristini. ISBN code: 978-88-93274289
Published by Luca Cristini Editore, via Orio 35/4- 24050 Zanica (BG) ITALY. www.soldiershop.com

UNIFORMS
OF THE RUSSIAN ARMY
DURING THE YEARS
1825-1855
VOL. 11

UNDER THE REIGN OF NICHOLAS I EMPEROUR OF
RUSSIA BETWEEN 1825 AND 1855

*

SERVICE TROOPS, MEDICAL, CIVILIAN & OTHERS

Russian soldiers of Preobrazhensky regiment

HISTORICAL DESCRIPTION OF THE CLOTHING AND ARMS
OF THE RUSSIAN ARMY - A.V. VISKOVATOV
(First English translation by Mark Conrad)

Soldiershop is glad to presents the complete collection of the great job made by A.V. Viskovatov dedicated to the uniforms and weapons belonging from the first Zar and Russian emperors to the Russian army during the Napoleonic period, until 1860 about. The time we considered in this volume corresponds to the reigns of Nicholas I that was the Emperor of Russia from 1825 until 1855. He was also the King of Poland and Grand Duke of Finland. He is best known as a political conservative whose reign was marked by geographical expansion, repression of dissent, economic stagnation, poor administrative policies, a corrupt bureaucracy, and frequent wars that culminated in Russia's defeat in the Crimean War of 1853–56.

Our reprint in based on the original 19th century volumes. This part is distributed at now on six volumes.

Our new edition, the first ever published in English, both on paper and digital format, boasts a large number of color plates, many of them unpublished and re-coloured by our team of expert artists and scholars of uniformology. Each volume is based on 100 color plates or more, always accompanied by the original translated text which describes the subjets of the plates.

A unique work in its genre, a must have in any respecting collection!

Aleksandr Vasilevich Viskovatov born 22 April (4 May New Style) 1804, died 27 February (11 March) 1858 in St. Petersburg, Russian military historian. He graduated from the 1st Cadet Corps and served in the artillery, the hydrographic depot of the Naval Ministry, and then in the Department of Military Educational Institutions. He mainly studied historical artifacts and the histories of military units. Viskovatov's greatest work was the Historical Description of the Clothing and Arms of the Russian Army (Vols. 1-30, St. Petersburg, 1841-62; 2nd ed. Vols. 1-34, St. Petersburg - Novosibirsk - Leningrad, 1899-1948). This work is based on a great quantity of archival documents and contains four thousand colored illustrations.

Viskovatov was the author of Chronicles of the Russian Army (Books 1-20, St. Petersburg, 1834-42) and Chronicles of the Russian Imperial Army (Parts 1-7, St. Petersburg, 1852). He collected valuable material on the history of the Russian navy which went into A Short Overview of Russian Naval Campaigns and General Voyages to the End of the XVII Century (St. Petersburg, 1864; 2nd edition Moscow, 1946). Together with A.I. Mikhailovskii-Danilevskii he helped prepare and create the Military Gallery in the Winter Palace. He wrote the historical military inscriptions for the walls of the Hall of St. George in the Great Palace of the Kremlin. (From the article in the Soviet Military Encyclopedia.)

CONTENTS

*

Preface pag. 5

*

HISTORICAL DESCRIPTION OF THE CLOTHING AND ARMS OF THE RUSSIAN ARMY

STAFF DUTY OFFICERS, OFFICERS ON SPECIAL DUTIES, SENIOR ADJUTANTS, GENERALS' ADJUTANTS, TOWN MAJORS, GATE MAJORS, TOWN AND BUILDINGS ADJUTANTS, PROVOSTS, WAGONMASTERS, UNATTACHED OFFICERS, THE CAMPAIGN STABLEMASTER, FELDJÄGERS, MINISTRY OF WAR OFFICIALS, MEDICAL OFFICIALS, GUARDS QUARTERMASTERS, AUDITORS, RIDING MASTERS, BANDMASTERS, ARMORERS, CIVILIAN OFFICIALS IN MILITARY EDUCATIONAL INSTITUTIONS, CANTONISTS AND THEIR OFFICERS, LOWER RANKS IN THE MINISTRY OF WAR AND EDUCATIONAL INSTITUTIONS, SERVICE COMPANIES IN EDUCATIONAL INSTITUTIONS, AND ORDERLIES. 1801 TO 1825.

LVII. STAFF DUTY OFFICERS. [*Dezhurnye Shtab-Ofitsery.*]

11 February 1826 – Staff Duty Officers' previous white cloth **pants** and high **boots** with buckled **spurs** are replaced by long dark-green pants and short boots worn under them, with driven-in spurs. For Staff Duty Officers at large in the Army or on the rolls of Infantry units these pants are ordered to have red piping (Illus. 977), but in the Separate Lithuanian Corps—raspberry piping. Those at large in the Cavalry or on the rolls of Cavalry units are to have wide red stripes and piping, but in the Lithuanian Corps—raspberry. For those in Garrison forces there is no piping (Illus. 978). Under no circumstances are these officers to wear any other kind of pants (1).

26 July 1826 - Staff Duty Officers in the Infantry arm are ordered, during summer, to wear white linen **pants** of the same pattern as those of dark-green cloth (Illus. 979). They are to be worn at those times when officers of troop units are prescribed to be in summer linen pants with gaiters (2).

1 January 1827 - In order to distinguish **rank** of Staff Duty Officers, they are ordered to have on their epaulettes small forged or stamped gold stars, as described above in detail for Grenader regiments (3).

13 October 1827 - Staff Duty Officers at large in the Light Cavalry or on the rolls of units prescribed to have **scaled epaulettes** are ordered to wear such epaulettes (4).

9 July 1829 – Staff Duty Officers in the Guards Cavalry, Guards Horse Artillery, Guards Horse Pioneers, and the 1st Lancer Division are ordered to wear dark-green **pants** with red stripes and piping, but when on campaign—grey riding trousers with red piping and no stripes. Officers in the Guards Cavalry and Horse Artillery stationed in the city of Warsaw, as well as in the Lithuanian Lancer Division, are to have dark-green pants and grey riding trousers with raspberry piping, without stripes. Those in the Army Cavalry, Army Horse Artillery, and Army Horse Pioneers—grey riding trousers with red piping, except for Staff Duty Officers in positions in the capital cities, who in those locations are prescribed dark-green pants with red stripes, and on campaign—grey riding trousers with red piping (5).

26 December 1829 - Uniform **buttons** for Staff Duty Officers in the Guards are ordered to have the same design as established at this time for the Guards, while those officers on the rolls of Army units or at large in the Army or Cavalry are to have buttons with a single-flame grenade (6).

25 November 1830 - The dark-green **pants** of all Staff Duty Officers in the Guards Cavalry are ordered to be without stripes, with only a single line of piping (7).

9 May 1831 - With the end of all exceptions to the general uniform regulations that existed for the former Separate Lithuanian Corps, **raspberry** stripes and piping are abolished for the uniforms of Staff Duty Officers who belonged to that corps (8).

8 June 1832 - All Staff Duty Officers are permitted to wear **moustaches** (9).

29 May 1836 - Staff Duty Officers are ordered to have **saddle girths** according to the branch of arms to which they belong (10).

15 July 1837 - Staff Duty Officers are given a new-pattern **sash**, with narrow silver lace rather the previous wide, with three stripes of light-orange and black silk, and tied round with its whole width between the two lowest coat buttons (11).

17 December 1837 - Staff Duty Officers are given **epaulettes** of a new pattern, with the addition of a fourth twist of thin cord (12).

23 January 1841 – The capes on Staff Duty Officers' **greatcoats** are ordered to be 1 arshin [28 inches] long, as measured from the lower edge of the collar (13).

18 April 1843 - When Staff Duty Officers are with a troop unit as part of their formation, they are ordered to wear the **hat** athwart, and not fore-and-aft (14).

2 January 1844 - Staff Duty Officers are ordered to have a **cockade** on the band of their forage caps, as established at this time for all branches and described in detail above for the uniforms of Grenadier regiments (15).

1 December 1844 - Instead of hats, Staff Duty Officers are ordered to wear **helmets** of the pattern introduced on 9 May of this year for combatant troops, with silvered mountings and a white horsehair plume: with the Guards helmet plate for those in the Guards, and for those in the Army—an Army plate with a single-flame grenade on the shield in front (Illus. 980) (16).

19 December 1844 - Staff Duty Officers of the **Corps of the Internal Guard** are given the same **helmets** as infantry Staff Duty Officers, but with a three-flame grenade in place of the plate (17).

13 October 1849 - Those in the Infantry and Foot Artillery are ordered to have infantry **half-sabers**, while those in the Heavy Cavalry are to wear **broadswords** with the sash, and cavalry **rapiers** when not wearing the sash (18).

15 February 1850 - Staff Duty Officers in the **Caucasus** are ordered to have uniforms of the patterns established for Caucasian Corps troops, namely:

Shapka headdress—top of dark-green cloth, trimmed along the four seams and lower edge with silver galloon with two narrow red stripes down the center.

Half-Caftan—the *parade* and *undress half-caftans* are similar in all respects to those for Generals of HIS MAJESTY'S Suite, with the only difference being that instead of embroidery on the collar and cuffs, these have silver buttonhole loops (on the parade half-caftan) and the buttons prescribed for this position (Illus. 981).

Sharavary pants—in place of the previous dark-green cloth pants, and instead of riding trousers—*sharavary* of gray-blue cloth, both being with red piping on the side seams.

Saber—of dragoon pattern, wholly identical to that for Generals of HIS IMPERIAL MAJESTY'S Suite (19).

LVIII. STAFF OFFICERS ASSIGNED TO MILITARY COMMANDERS FOR SPECIAL DUTIES.

[*Shtab-Ofitsery, sostoyashchie dlya osobykh poruchenii pri voinskikh nachal'nikakh.*]

10 Februay 1826 – Staff Officers assigned to military commanders for special duties, if they are not unattached in the Army or Cavalry but rather are on the rolls of a regiment, are to wear the **uniform** prescribed for Staff Duty Officers (20). Following this, all the changes in uniform which Staff Duty Officers underwent also applied to them.

LIX. SENIOR ADJUTANTS and GENERALS' ADJUTANTS. [*Starshie i general'skie ad"yutanty.*]

11 February 1826 – These Adjutants' previous white cloth **pants** with high **boots** and buckled **spurs** are replaced with long dark-green pants and short boots worn under the pants, with driven-in spurs. Adjutants at large in the Army or on the rolls of Infantry units are ordered to have these pants with red piping (Illus. 982), and those in the Separate Lithuanian Corps—with raspberry piping. Those unattached in the Cavalry or on the rolls of a Cavalry regiment have red piping (Illus. 982), but raspberry stripes and piping if in the Lithuanian Corps. Adjutants in Garrison forces have no piping. All these officers are not to wear any other pants under any circumstances (21).

1 January 1827 - Senior and Generals' Adjutants, in order to distinguish **rank**, are ordered to have small stamped or forged gold **stars** on their epaulettes, as described above in detail for Grenadier regiments (23).

13 October 1827 - Senior and Generals' Adjutants in the Light Cavalry and belonging to units prescribed **scaled epaulettes** are ordered to also wear such epaulettes (24).

19 May 1829 – When wearing the sash and in formation, Senior and Generals' Adjutants in the Heavy Cavalry are ordered to carry the **broadsword** [*palash*] on the silver swordbelt prescribed for Adjutants of Light Cavalry, but in other situations they are to have, as before, the cavalry **rapier** (25).

9 July 1829 – Senior and Generals' Adjutants in the Guards Cavalry, Guards Horse Artillery, Guards Horse Pioneers, and 1st Lancer Division are ordered to wear dark-green **pants** with red stripes and piping, and when on campaign—grey **riding trousers** with red piping and no stripes. Those in the Guards Cavalry and Horse Artillery located in the city of Warsaw, as well as those in the Lithuanian Lancer Division, are to have dark-green pants and grey riding trousers with raspberry piping without stripes. For those in the Army Cavalry, Army Horse Artillery, and Army Horse Pioneers—grey riding trousers with red piping (Illus. 983), except for Senior and Generals' Adjutants on duties in the capital cities, who in these places are prescribed dark-green pants with red stripes, but on campaign—grey riding trousers with red piping (26).

26 December 1829 – The **buttons** on the uniforms of Senior and Generals' Adjutants who are in the Guards are ordered to have the same design as established at this time for the Guards, while those Adjutants in Army units or unattached in the Army and Cavalry are to have buttons with a single-flame grenade (27).

25 November 1830 – Senior and Generals' Adjutants from Guards Cavalry units are ordered to have dark-green **pants** with a single line of red piping, without any stripes (28).

9 May 1831 – With the elimination of all the exceptions to general uniform regulations that existed for the former Separate Lithuanian Corps, the raspberry color for **stripes and piping** on the uniforms for Senior and Generals' Adjutants from this Corps is also abolished (29).

8 June 1832 – All Senior and Generals' Adjutants are allowed to wear **moustaches** (30).

29 May 1836 – Senior and Generals' Adjutants are ordered to have to have **saddle girths** according to the branch of service to which they belong (31).

15 July 1837 – Senior and Generals' Adjutants are given a new-pattern **sash** with a narrow silver lace band instead of the previous wide one, with three stripes of light-orange and black silk. The sash is worn with its entire width fitting between the two lowest buttons of the coat (32) .

17 December 1837 – Senior and Generals' Adjutants are given **epaulettes** of a new pattern with an additional fourth thin twist of cord (33).

23 January 1841 – **Greatcoat** capes for Senior and Generals' Adjutants are ordered to be 1 arshin [28 inches] long as measured from the lower end of the collar (34).

18 April 1843 – Senior and Generals' Adjutants, when with troop units as part of their formation, are ordered to wear the **hat** athwart, and not fore-and-aft (35).

2 January 1844 – Senior and Generals' Adjutants are ordered to have a **cockade** on the front of the band of their forage caps, as established at this same time for all branches and described above in detail for the uniform for Grenadier regiments (36).

1 December 1844 – In place of hats, Senior and Generals' Adjutants are ordered to have wear **helmets** of the pattern introduced on 9 May of this year for combatant troops, with silvered mountings and a white hair plume. For those in the Guards—with a Guards plate (Illus. 984), and in the Army—an Army plate, with a single-flame grenade on the front in the shield (37).

19 December 1844 – Senior and Generals' Adjutants in the **Internal Guard** are given the exact same **helmets** as Staff Duty Officers of the Internal Guard, i.e. with a three-flame grenade in place of a helmet plate (Illus. 985) (38).

13 October 1849 - Senior and Generals' Adjutants of the Infantry and Foot Artillery are ordered to wear infantry **half-sabers** instead of rapiers; those in the Heavy Cavalry are to be with a **broadsword** when wearing the sash, and with a cavalry **rapier** when not wearing a sash (39).

15 February 1850 - Senior and Generals' Adjutants in the **Caucasus** are ordered to have uniforms of the patterns established for troops of the Separate Caucasian Corps and identical to the uniforms of Staff Duty Officers (40).

18 February 1854 – Cavalry and Infantry Adjutants are ordered to acquire **horse furniture** according to the following descriptions:

1.) For those in the Light Cavalry, saddle and other iterms the exact same as throughout the Light Cavalry; saddlecloths of black lambskin with slit flaps cut out in front from which to draw out the pistols; towards the rear arch of the saddle, 1-1/4 inches below the bronze edge, an iron bracket is attached in order to strap the valise to the arch itself and thus lift it off the horse's back. The valise is exactly as for cavalry officers, and the campaign greatcoat is stowed on the front arch under the saddlecloth. However, Adjutants from regiments in the Guards Cuirassier Division are to have horse furniture of the pattern for cuirassiers.

2.) With English saddles the saddlecloth stays the same without any changes except that it is to be made 1 vershok [1-3/4 inches] longer in the rear, and in the front have slit flaps cut out through which the pistols may be drawn from their holders. Behind the saddle is a valise of grey-blue cloth, as for Guards Cuirassiers, and the campaign greatcoat is stowed over the saddlecloth in a leather case (41).

29 April 1854 - In wartime Adjutants are ordered to have campaign **greatcoats** like those established at this time for Army and Guards troops, with white piping on the collar and shoulder straps (42).

LX. TOWN MAJORS, GATE MAJORS, BUILDINGS ADJUTANT, AND TOWN ADJUTANTS.
[Plats-Maiory, Maiory-ot-Vorot i Bau i Plats-Ad"yutanty.]

11 February 1826 – The currently worn white cloth **pants** and high **boots** with buckled-on spurs worn by Town Majors, Gate Majors, and Town and Buildings Adjutants are replaced with dark-green pants with short boots worn under them, with driven-in spurs. Town Majors, Gate Majors, and Town and Buildings Adjutants unattached in the Army or in the Infantry are to have orange piping on the pants (Illus. 986), while those at large in the Cavalry or on the rolls of Cavalry units are to additionally have orange stripes (Illus. 986) (43).

26 July 1826 – Town Majors, Gate Majors, and Town and Buildings Adjutants from the Infantry are ordered to wear white linen **pants** in summer, of the same pattern as the dark-green cloth pants (Illus. 987), and wearing them at the same times as combatant officers are prescribed to be in summer linen pants with gaiters (44).

1 January 1827 – In order to distinguish **rank**, Town Majors, Gate Majors, and Town and Buildings Adjutants are ordered to have stamped or forged gold stars on their epaulettes, as described above in detail for Grenadier regiments (45).

13 October 1827 – Town Majors, Gate Majors, and Town and Buildings Adjutants at large in the Light Cavalry or on the rolls of those units that are prescribed scaled epaulettes are ordered to wear such epaulettes (46).

9 July 1829 – Town Majors, Gate Majors, and Town and Buildings Adjutants from the Guards Cavalry, Guards Horse Artillery, Guards Horse Pioneers, and the 1st Lancer Division, as well as those unattached from the Army Cavalry, Army Horse Artillery, and Army Horse Pioneers, and assigned to positions in the capital cities are ordered to wear dark-green **pants** with orange stripes and piping. All others not assigned to such positions are to have pants without stripes and only piping (47).

29 December 1829 – Town Majors, Gate Majors, and Town and Buildings Adjutants from the Guards are to have uniform **buttons** with the same design as established at this time for the Guards, while those from Army units or at large in the Army and Cavalry branches are to have buttons with a single-flame grenade (48).

25 November 1830 – All Town Majors, Gate Majors, and Town and Buildings Adjutants from the Cavalry are ordered to have dark-green **pants** with only a single line of orange piping and no stripes (49).

8 June 1832 – All Town Majors, Gate Majors, and Town and Buildings Adjutants may wear **moustaches** (50).

15 July 1837 – Town Majors, Gate Majors, and Town and Buildings Adjutants are given a new-pattern **sash**, being a narrow silver lace band instead of the previous wide one, with three stripes of light-orange and black silk, worn around the body so that its entire width is between the two bottom coat buttons (51).

17 December 1837 – Town Majors, Gate Majors, and Town and Buildings Adjutants are given new-pattern **epauletts**, with an additional fourth thin twist of cord (52).

23 January 1841 – The capes on **greatcoats** of Town Majors, Gate Majors, and Town and Buildings Adjutants are to be 1 arshin [28-inches] long as measured from the bottom edge of the collar (53).

18 April 1843 – When with troops as part of one of their formations, Town Majors, Gate Majors, and Town and Buildings Adjutants are to wear the **hat** athwart [*pryamo*] and not fore-and-aft [*s polya*] (54).

29 December 1843 – Gate Majors of the new **Kremlin Palace** in Moscow are ordered to have silver **embroidered edging** on the coat's collar and cuffs, and buttonhole loops of the same (55).

2 January 1844 – Town Majors, Gate Majors, and Town and Buildings Adjutants are to have a **cockade** on the front of the band of the forage cap, as laid down for all arms and described above in detail for the uniforms of Grenadier regiments (56).

7 August 1849 – In place of hats, all officers in these positions are given **helmets** of the pattern introduced on 9 May 1844 for combatant troops, with silvered mountings and a black hair plume. Those from the Guards have a Guards pattern plate, while those in Army have a single-flame grenade on the shield in front (Illus. 988) (57).

13 October 1849 – Town Majors, Gate Majors, and Town and Buildings Adjutants from the Infantry and Foot Artillery are to carry infantry **half-sabers**, while those from the Heavy Cavalry are to have **broadswords** when wearing the sash and cavalry **rapiers** when not wearing the sash (58).

15 February 1850 – Town Majors and Town and Buildings Adjutants in the **Caucasus** are ordered to have uniforms exactly like those given at this time to Adjutants and Staff Duty Officers, with the color orange substituted for red (59).

LXI. PROVOSTS. [*Geval'digery.*]

11 February 1826 – In place of their previous double-breasted dress coat, provosts [*geval'digery*, from the German *Gewaltiger* - M.C.] are ordered to have single-breasted **coats** (with nine buttons on front), with white piping down the front and from the front to the turn-backs, and instead of white cloth pants and high boots with buckled-on spurs, they are to wear long dark-green **pants** with sky-blue piping and short **boots** worn under the pants, with driven-in spurs (Illus. 989) (60).

26 July 1826 – Provosts from the Infantry are ordered to wear linen white **pants** in summertime, of the same pattern as the dark-green cloth pants (Illus. 990). These are to be worn in those circumstances in which combatant officers are prescribed to be in linen summer pants with gaiters (61).

1 January 1827 – In order to distinguish **rank**, Provosts are ordered to have small stamped or forged gold stars on the epaulettes, as described above in detail for Grenadier regiments (62).

13 October 1827 – Provosts from the Light Cavalry are ordered to have silver scaled **epaulettes** of the same pattern as established at this time for Light Cavalry regiments (63).

26 December 1829 – Provosts from Guards units are ordered to have uniform **buttons** with the same design as established at this time for the Guards, while those from Army units or unattached in the Army or Cavalry are to have buttons with a single-flame grenade (64).

8 June 1832 – All Provosts are authorized to wear **moustaches** (65).

15 July 1837 – Provosts are given a new-pattern **sash** with a narrow silver belt of silver lace instead of the previous wide one, with three stripes of light-orange and black silk, and wrapped around the body so that its entire width is between the two bottom coat buttons (66).

17 December 1837 – Provosts are given **epauletts** of the new pattern with an additional fourth thin twist of cord (67).

23 January 1841 – The capes on the **greatcoats** of Provosts are to be 1 arshin [28-inches] long as measured from the bottom edge of the collar (68).

2 January 1844 – Provosts are ordered to have a **cockade** on the front of the forage cap band, as established at this time in the Army in general and described above in detail for the uniforms of Grenadier regiments (69).

7 December 1844 – Instead of hats, Provosts are given **helmets** of the pattern established for combatant troops on 9 May of this year. Provosts' helmets are to be of the style of the branch of service to which they belong. Appointments and plumes are to be white (70).

13 October 1849 – Provosts in the Infantry or Foot Artillery are ordered to have **half-sabers**, while those in the Heavy Cavalry are to have **broadswords** when wearing the sash and cavalry **rapiers** when not wearing the sash (71).

15 February 1850 – Provosts in the **Caucasus** are ordered to have uniforms of the Caucasus Corps pattern, the same as for Staff Duty Officers with the color red changed to sky blue (72).

29 April 1854 – In wartime it is ordered to have campaign greatcoats (73).

LXII. WAGON MASTERS. [*Vagenmeistery.*]

11 February 1826 – The previous white cloth pants and high boots with buckled-on spurs of Wagon Masters are replaced with long dark-green **pants** with sky-blue stripes and piping and short **boots** worn under the pants, with driven-in spurs (Illus. 991) (74).

1 January 1827 – In order to distinguish **rank**, Wagon Masters are ordered to have small stamped or forged gold stars on the epalettes, as described above in detail for Grenadier regiments (75).

13 October 1827 – Wagon Masters from the Light Cavalry are ordered to have silver scaled **epaulettes** of the same pattern as established at this time for Light Cavalry regiments (76).

26 December 1829 – Wagon Masters from Guards units are ordered to have uniform **buttons** with the same design as established at this time for the Guards, while those from Army units or unattached in the Army or Cavalry are to have buttons with a single-flame grenade (77).

25 November 1830 – Wagon Masters are ordered to have pants without stripes, with only a single line of sky-blue piping, as before (78).

8 June 1832 – All Wagon Masters are allowed to wear **moustaches** (79).

15 July 1837 – Wagon Masters are given a new-pattern **sash** with a narrow silver belt of silver lace instead of the previous wide one, with three stripes of light-orange and black silk, and wrapped around the body so that its entire width is between the two bottom coat buttons (80).

17 December 1837 – Wagon Masters are given **epauletts** of the new pattern with an additional fourth thin twist of cord (81).

23 January 1841 – The capes on Wagon Masters' **greatcoats** are to be 1 arshin [28-inches] long as measured from the bottom edge of the collar (82).

2 January 1844 – Wagon Masters are ordered to have a **cockade** on the front of the forage cap band, as established at this time throughout the Army and described above in detail for the uniforms of Grenadier regiments (83).

7 December 1844 – Instead of hats, Wagon Masters are given **helmets** of the pattern established for combatant troops on 9 May of this year. The helmet is to be of the style for the branch of service to which the Wagon Master belongs; mountings and plume are white (Illus. 992) (84).

Additionally, the directives for Provosts from **13 October 1849**, **15 February 1850**, and **29 April 1854** are also applied to Wagon Masters.

LXIII. FIELD AND COMPANY-GRADE OFFICERS UNATTACHED IN THE ARMY AND CAVALRY.

[*Shtab i Ober-Ofitsery, sostoyashchie po Armii i Kavalerii.*]

11 February 1826 – The previous double-breasted dress coat of Field-Grade Officers at large in the Army is ordered replaced with single-breasted **coats** (with nine buttons in front), with red piping down the front opening, from the front to the skirts, and on the turnbacks. Instead of white cloth pants and high boots with buckled-on spurs, they are to wear long dark-green **pants** with red piping and short **boots** worn under the pants, with driven-in spurs (Illus. 993). Field and Company-Grade Officers at large in the Cavalry are prescribed the same pants but with the addition of red stripes (Illus. 994) (85).

26 July 1826 - Field and Company-Grade Officers at large in the Army are ordered, during summer, to wear white linen **pants** of the same pattern as those of dark-green cloth (Illus. 995). They are to be worn at those times when officers of troop units are prescribed to be in summer linen pants with gaiters (86).

1 January 1827 - In order to distinguish **rank** of Field and Company-Officers at large in the Army and Cavalry, they are ordered to have on their epaulettes small forged or stamped silver stars, as described above in detail for Grenader regiments (87).

13 October 1827 - Field and Company-Grade Officers at large in the Light Cavalry are ordered to wear scaled **epaulettes** of the pattern established at this time for regiments of Light Cavalry and described above in detail for Dragoon regiments (88).

9 July 1829 – Field and Company-Grade Officers at large in the Cavalry are ordered to wear grey **riding trousers** with red piping on all occasions except when on duties in the capital cities, when they are to be in dark-green pants with red stripes and piping (89).

26 December 1829 - Field and Company-Grade Officers at large in the Army and Cavalry are ordered to have uniform **buttons** with a single-flame grenade, as established at this time for Army troops (90).

25 November 1830 - Field and Company-Grade Officers at large in the Cavalry and on duties in the capital cities are ordered to wear dark-green **riding trousers** with red piping and no stripes (91).

8 June 1832 - All Field and Company-Grade Officers at large in the Army and Cavalry are permitted to wear **moustaches** (92).

15 July 1837 - Field and Company-Grade Officers at large in the Army and Cavalry are given a new-pattern **sash**, with narrow silver lace rather the previous wide, with three stripes of light-orange and black silk, and tied round with its whole width between the two lowest coat buttons (93).

17 December 1837 - Field and Company-Grade Officers at large in the Army and Cavalry are given **epaulettes** of a new pattern, with the addition of a fourth twist of thin cord (94).

23 January 1841 – The capes on the **greatcoats** of Field and Company-Grade Officers at large in the Army and Cavalry are ordered to be 1 arshin [28 inches] long, as measured from the lower edge of the collar (95).

2 January 1844 - Field and Company-Grade Officers at large in the Army and Cavalry are ordered to have a **cockade** on the band of their forage caps, as established at this time for all branches and described in detail above for the uniforms of Grenadier regiments (96).

30 April 1846 - Field-Grade Officers at large in the Army, Cavalry, or Artillery, when commanding regiments or other troop units, are ordered to have a **uniform** of the pattern for that unit which they command (97).

4 November 1846 - Commanders of **Fortress Artillery** administrations [*Komandiry Krepostnykh Artilleriiskikh Upravlenii*] at large in the

Artillery are ordered to have the same uniform as prescribed for the Garrison Artillery officers subordinate to them, with the only difference being that Commanders of such administrations, not being part of any particular company, have epaulettes with a blank silver field (98).

20 June 1849 - In place of hats, Field-Grade Officers at large in the Army, Cavalry, or Artillery are ordered to have **helmets** with a gold plate as established for Grenadiers, without a number on the grenade but with a plume: white for those in the Cavalry and black for those in the Army or Artillery (Illus. 996) (99).

13 October 1849 - Those in the Infantry and Foot Artillery are ordered to have infantry **half-sabers** instead of rapiers (Illus. 996) (100).

20 October 1849 - **Police Commandants** [*Politsiimeistery*] from the Army and Cavalry are ordered by HIGHEST Authority to have: *helmets* with white fittings, a Grenadier plate, and a black hair plume; dark-green cloth *dress coat* of the pattern for Town Majors, with a dark-green collar and orange piping; cuff flaps are orange for the capital cities and dark green with orange piping otherwise; silver buttonhole loops on the collar and cuff flaps; silvered buttons with a single-flame grenade (Illus. 997); orange lining; *pants* and *frock coat* are of the same cloth as the dress coat, with orange piping (101).

31 October 1849 - As a supplement to Order No. 106 of 20 October 1849, HIGHEST Authority orders that **Town Commandants** [*Gorodnichie*] from the Army and Cavalry are prescribed the same uniforms as established for Police Commandants, with the Town Commandants to have dark-green cuff with orange piping (102).

22 December 1849 - HIGHEST Confirmation is given to a description of the uniform for military Field-Grade Officers at large in the Army and Cavalry and serving in the **Caucasus** or **Trans-Caucasus** territories by holding the various **police positions** there, such as: Police Commandants, Town Commandants, District and Regional Chiefs, their Deputies, Sector Chiefs and Assistants, their Deputies, Constables and their Police Deputies, Commissars, etc. [*Politsiimeistery, Gorodnichie, Uezdnye i Okruzhnye Nachal'niki, ikh Pomoshchniki, Uchastkovye Nachal'niki i Zasedateli, ikh Pomoshchniki, Pristavy i ikh Pomoshchniki Politseiskie, Kommisary, i t.p.*]

Shapka headdress—of the pattern for Caucasus troops, with a dark-green cloth top and silver galloon, without any color in the galloon.

Half-Caftan [Polukaftan]—of dark-green cloth with dark-green collar and cuffs. Orange piping along the collar, cuffs, front, and skirts. Silver buttonhole loops on the collar and cuffs. Silvered buttons with a single-flame grenade. Orange lining.

Sharavary pants—dark-green cloth with orange piping. Instead of a frock coat, a half-caftan of the same pattern but without buttonhole loops.

Sword belt [Portupeya]—for sabers and infantry half-sabers, over the shoulder, lined with silver galloon (103).

15 February 1850 - Unattached officers in the Army, Cavalry, and Artillery in the **Caucasus** are ordered to have uniforms of the patterns established for the troops of the Separate Caucasian Corps, namely:

Shapka headdress in the Caucasian style; its top of dark-green cloth, trimmed with gold galloon down the middle of which are two narrow red stripes.

Half-Caftan instead of the tail coat and frock; it has the same collar as was on the tail coat. For officers in the Army and Cavalry the cuffs are of the same cloth as the half-caftan, while for those in the Artillery they are of black cloth. Red piping down the front and on the skirts, around the upper edge of the cuffs, and on the pocket flaps.

Sharavary pants of dark-green cloth for officers in the Army and Artillery, and of grey-blue cloth with red trim for those in the Cavalry.

Saber of dragoon pattern, on a sword belt of gold galloon with gold fittings and lined with black morocco; with a cavalry-pattern sword knot for officers in the Cavalry and an infantry-pattern one for the rest (104).

19 April 1850 - Officers of the Army, Cavalry, and Artillery holding positions in St. Petersburg as Inspectors of city prisons and the Correctional Institution [*Ispravitel'noe Zavedenie*], as well as their Assistants, are ordered to wear **helmets** instead of hats (105).

30 November 1850 - Officers attached to Military Governors and Governor Generals for special duties, as well as all Field and Company-Grade Officers holding positions in the Civil administration, are ordered to wear, instead of hats, **helmets** with a gold Grenadier-pattern plate without a number on the grenade, and with white hair plumes for those in the Cavalry and black for others. This regulation is not extended to officers holding police positions in the Caucasus or Trans-Caucasus, who are prescribed their own headdress (106).

LXIV. THE MILITARY CAMPAIGN STABLE MASTER IN HIS IMPERIAL MAJESTY'S MAIN HEADQUARTERS.

[*Voenno-Pokhodnyi Shtalmeister Glavnago Shtaba EGO IMPERATORSKAGO VELICHESTVA.*]

2 August 1836 – For the position of **Military Campaign Stable Master in HIS IMPERIAL MAJESTY'S Main Headquarters**, established on 31 July of this year, there is prescribed the same uniform as for the Wagon Master-General in HIS IMPERIAL MAJESTY'S Main Headquarters, i.e. a dark-green tail coat with sky-blue collar, cuff flaps, and lining to the coat and epaulettes; white piping on the collar, cuffs, cuff flaps, down the front, on the turnbacks, and on the pocket flaps; with silver buttons and silver standard embroidery on the collar, cuffs, and cuff flaps (Illus. 998); dark-green pants and grey riding trousers—one and the other with sky-blue piping, but for parades white cloth pants, and with them: Hussar boots if the Stable Master is from the Light Cavalry, and high jackboots [*botforty*] if from the Heavy. Collars on the frock coat and greatcoat are piped white, and the same piping is on the frock coat's cuffs and pocket flaps. Forage cap with a sky-blue cap band and white piping around the band's edges and the top of the cap. Epaulettes are ordered to be according to rank, and weapons according to branch of service. Thus, the first Stable Master for Military Campaigns, a lieutenant-colonel from the Light Cavalry, carried a saber on a sword belt lined with silver galloon (107).

2 January 1844 - The Stable Master for Military Campaigns is ordered to have a **cockade** on the front of his forage cap band, as established at this time for all branches and described above in detail under uniforms for Grenadier regiments (108).

7 December 1844 - The Stable Master for Military Campaigns is ordered to wear a cavalry helmet with a silver Guards plate and mountings, a gilt IMPERIAL monogram on the shield of the plates, and a white plume (Illus. 999) (109).

4 January 1845 - This helmet is ordered to have, on the right side under the chinscales, a metallic cockade, as established at this time for generals and field and company-grade officers in line units (110).

LXV. FELDJÄGERS. [*Fel'd''egerya.*]

26 May 1826 – For Feldjäger officers and Feldjägers [the tsar's official couriers and messangers - M.C.], the previous double-breasted dress coat with red collar and cuffs is ordered replaced with a single-breasted coat with nine buttons in front, a dark-green collar piped red, and the same piping on the coattails. Left as before are the red cuffs, dark-grey riding trousers—but with no stripes on the latter and only a single row of piping, and short boots with driven-in spurs (Illus. 1000) (111). The frock coat's collar and cuffs are prescribed to be dark green with red piping, while the greatcoat collar is to be grey with the same red piping. When on the road, officers as well as feldjägers are ordered to have a saber on a black sword belt (Illus. 1001), and wear a dark-green forage cap with the same colored band and red piping: for officers—on the upper and lower edges of the band and around the top of the crown, and for feldjägers—only around the band's edges (Illus. 1001) (112 [sic-M.C.]).

1 January 1827 - In order to distinguish **rank** of field and company-officers in the Feldjäger Corps, they are ordered to have on their epaulettes small stamped silver stars, as established for all other field and company-grade officers in the military establishment (112).

8 June 1832 - Feldjäger officers and Feldjägers are permitted to wear **moustaches** (113).

2 January 1844 - Field and Company-Grade Officers of the Feldjäger Corps are ordered to have a **cockade** on the band of their forage caps, as established at this time for all branches (114).

14 March 1845 - In place of hats, Feldjäger officers and Feldjägers are ordered to have **helmets** of the pattern newly introduced in the forces: officers with gilt mountings and a cockade after the example of Army officers, while Feldjägers are to have brass mountings, without gilt, of the pattern for lower ranks. All are to have a white hair plume and a metal edge around the helmet's front visor (Illus. 1002). Plates on these helmets are to have, cut out on the front of the shield, a HIGHEST monogram under an IMPERIAL crown (Illus. 1003) (115).

13 October 1849 - The ranks of the Feldjäger Corps are ordered to have infantry **half-sabers** instead of rapiers (116).

LXVI. MILITARY AND CIVILIAN OFFICIALS OF HIS IMPERIAL MAJESTY'S MAIN HEADQUARTERS AND WAR MINISTRY.
[*Voennye i klassnye chinovniki Glavnago Shtaba EGO IMPERATORSKAGO VELICHESTVA i Voennago Ministerstva.*]

11 February 1826 – Instead of short pants with high boots, civilian officials of HIS IMPERIAL MAJESTY'S Main Headquarters and War Ministry are ordered to wear long dark-green **pants** without piping, and short with driven-in spurs. For parade occasions, officials of class 5 and higher retain their white cloth pants and jackboots with spurs (117).

26 February 1826 – All the above mentioned officials are ordered to have **coats** with nine (instead of six) buttons on the front. With this, officials of HIS IMPERIAL MAJESTY'S Main Headquarters keep their cuffs with flaps: in the Military Topography Depot - blue [*svetlosinii*], and in other departments - red, while in the War Ministry the cuffs are without flaps (Illus. 1004, 1005, and 1006) (118).

4 March 1834 - HIGHEST Authority confirms the following regulations regarding **uniforms** for military and civilian officials of the War Ministry, under which as of 1 May 1832 came the Departments and other offices of HIS IMPERIAL MAJESTY'S Main Headquarters:

1.) All War Ministry officials, military as well as civilian, are to have the same uniform coat of military cut.

2.) Military officials are to wear this uniform with military appurtenances, and civilian officials without.

3.) All military ranks are to have coats with the same embroidery, but in regard to the wearing of embroidery, civilian officials are divided into categories [*razryady*] according to their duties, as is the procedure in all Ministries.

4.) The new uniform is now prescribed to be worn by: a) all higher ranks without exception; b) officials of the Ministry's Chancellery, also without exception; c) all newly appointed officials in the Departments, without exception, with the assumption that the selection of these officials will be carried out with due care, and d) of currently serving officials in the Departments, only those who will be singled out as deserving, as a mark of distinction, upon nomination by Directors and confirmation by the Minister.

5.) A general distinction of the coat for officials of the Ministry's central administration, as opposed to those in subordinate departments, is that for the former embroidery is prescribed to be with an edge [*s kantom*], cuff flaps red, and buttons with the image of the state coat-of-arms. and officials belonging to the category 1 by virtue of their duties have, instead of epaulettes, silver shoulder straps made of general officers' cord [*general'skaya kanitel'*]. For the officials in subordinate departments the embroidery has no edging, cuff flaps are green with red piping, and buttons are according to a special design, while officials of category 1 have shoulder straps made from field-grade officers' cord.

6.) All medical and auditor officials in the forces keep their previous uniforms, but civilian officials in the Auditors' and Medical Departments who do not have auditor or medical positions are to wear the new coat, the same as officials in other Departments.

7.) When officials are discharged into full retirement, the right to wear the new uniform is to be granted, at the Minister of War's discretion, only to those who held officer rank for 10 years and in that time served with distinction not less than 3 years in the War Ministry's Departments.

8.) The right to wear the new uniform is not extended to officials who left the military administration before the introduction of this uniform. The uniforms themselves are established with the following particulars:

A.) War Ministry officials, military as well as civilian, have a coat of the same military cut, dark green with red cloth collar and similar piping on the skirts; green piping on the collar, dark-green cuffs with red flaps and green piping; dark-green lining; dark-green pants with red piping; boots with spurs. Silver embroidery according to the design now in use, and hollow [*dutyi*] silver buttons with an image of the state coat-of-arms.

B.) Military officials are to wear this uniform with military appurtenances according to their arm of service, and have, for all without distinction, straight silver buttonhole loops on the collar and cuff flaps, surrounded by matching silver edging (Illus. 1007 and 1008).

C.) Civilian officials have a rapier [*shpaga*] with this uniform, with a silver sword knot, and a tricorn hat without plume. In regard to the fullness of the embroidery, it is divided into five categories corresponding to the duties of the position being held.

D.) Belonging to the *first category* are:

a.) Directors of Departments and the War Ministry Chancellery.

b.) The Senior Official of HIS IMPERIAL MAJESTY'S Military Campaign Chancellery.

c.) Intendant-General of the Army.

These officials have full embroidery on the collar, cuffs, cuff flaps, and pockets, i.e. in addition to the straight silver buttonhole loops there is a silver border and edge [*bort i kant*] (Illus. 1009, 1010, and 1011). Instead of epaulettes they have shoulder straps of silver general officers' cord (Illus. 1009 and 1012), and, on ceremonial days, white pants with jackboots are worn with this coat.

E.) Belonging to the *second category* are:

a.) Vice-Directors of War Ministry Departments.

b.) Officials assigned to the Minister of War and the Ministry ranking not lower than class 5.

They have only edging on the pocket flaps; embroidery on the collar, cuffs, and cuff flaps is the same as for the 1st category (Illus. 1009). In addition, Vice-Directors have shoulder straps of silver general officers' cord, the same as Directors.

F.) Belonging to the *third category* are:

a.) Section Chiefs [*Nachal'niki Otdelenii*] in War Ministry Departments and the Chancellery.

b.) Junior Officials of HIS IMPERIAL MAJESTY'S Military Campaign Chancellery.

c.) Chiefs of Archives and Chancellery Heads in the Departments.

d.) Officials assigned to the Minister of War and the Ministry of field and company-grade officer rank.

e.) Administrative Director of the Military Academic Committee [*Pravitel' del Voenno-Uchenago Komiteta*].

These officials have: full embroidery on the collar; edging and buttonhole loops on the cuff flaps, and on the cuffs—only edging (Illus. 1013); on the pockets there is no embroidery at all. (*Note: Because on 6 April 1836, before this Regulation went into effect, the full embroidery on coats for this category was removed, leaving only edging and buttonhole loops, Illustration 1013 is drawn in conformance with that change.*)

G.) Belonging to the fourth category are:

a.) Secretaries, Bookkeepers, and the Executor, Archivist, and Translator in the War Ministry Chancellery.

b.) Secretaries, Office Chiefs, Translators, Archivists, Treasurers, Executors, Bookkeepers and Comptrollers, both senior and junior, and Deputies to Chancellery Directors and Archive Chiefs in War Ministry Departments.

c.) Academic Secretaries of the Military Academic Committee.

d.) Officials of company-grade officer rank assigned to Departments for special duties.

These officials have silver buttonhole loops on the collar and cuff flaps, with silver edging (Illus. 1013). < fontsize="3">(*Note: Because on 6 April 1836, before this Regulation went into effect, the cuff flaps on coats for officials of this category were ordered to have only buttonhole loops and no edging, Illustration 1013 is drawn in conformance with that change.*)

H.) Belonging to the *fifth category* are;

a.) Journalists and Assistants to Secretaries and Bookkeepers, in the War Ministry Chancellery.

b.) Assistants to Secretaries, Office Chiefs, Archivists, Treasurers, Exectutors, Bookkeepers, and Comptrollers, and Journalists, in War Ministry Departments.

c.) Journalists and Assistants to Academic Secretaries, of the Military Academic Committee.

These officials have silver buttonhole loops and edging only on the collar (Illus. 1014).

I.) All War Ministry officials have undress coats [*vitse-mundiry*] for everyday use at work, the same as the dress coat but without embroidery. They can also have a frock coat of the normal military pattern, dark green with a red cloth collar piped green, red piping on the cuffs and pockets, and silver buttons the same as on the dress coat (Illus. 1015 and 1016).

J.) Military and civilian officials in offices under War Ministry Departments, as well as in Intendance Bureaus, are prescribed the same uniform but with embroidery without silver edging, with green cuff flaps piped red (Illus. 1017, 1018, and 1019), and with buttons with the following designs:

a.) For civilian officials on the Staffs of Guards forces or in Guards regiments—with the Guards design.

b.) For officials of all offices and agencies subordinate to War Ministry Departments (except for the Artillery Department), and on the Staffs of all other forces, Intendance Bureaus, and Field Provisioning agencies not mentioned below—with a single-flame grenade.

c.) For officials in offices and agencies under the Artillery Department—with the same grenade and two cannons.

d.) For officials of Military Educational Institutions and their Staffs and Advisory Boards—with the design prescribed for Military Educational Institutions, i.e. similar to their shako plate.

e.) For officials in regiments or various units, buttons are directed to be with those designs prescribed for these regiments and units by existing regulations (119).

6 April 1834 - It is directed by HIGHEST Authority:

1.) Field and company-grade officers of the General Staff and Corps of Topographers, as well as Artillery and Engineer officers, occupying official positions in War Ministry Departments, are to wear the **uniform** established by HIGHEST Authority through the Regulation of 4 March of this year for officials of this Ministry, and not to use the uniform of that branch of service to which they belong. The Quartermaster-General in HIS IMPERIAL MAJESTY'S Main Headquarters, the Artillery and Engineering Departamental Directors, the Vice-Directors of these Departments who hold general-officer rank, and the Director and Members of the Military Academic Committee are given the opportunity to wear the War Ministry uniform in addition to that of the branch of service to which they belong.

2.) Section Chiefs and all civilian officials who by the aforementioned Regulation must wear a uniform with 3rd category embroidery are not to have an embroidered border on the collar, but rather to have only buttonhole loops and edging.

3.) Officials who by the same Regulation have 4th category embroidery are not to have edging on the cuff flaps, but only buttonhole loops (120).

6 June 1834 - Generals and Field and Company-Grade Officers who by the directives of 4 March and 6 April of this year are prescribed the uniforms established for War Ministry officials are ordered to wear with them the military appurtenances appropriate to the branch of service to which the Generals and Field and Company-Grade Officers belong, i.e. for those from the Heavy Cavalry—**broadswords** and **hats** with white plumes; from the Light Cavalry—**sabers** and also hats with white plumes, but in the rest of the branches—infantry **swords** and hats with black plumes.

Along with this, all Generals and Field and Company-Grade Officers, military as well as civilian officials, are to wear white summer **pants** with the War Ministry coats, in agreement with their usage in the field forces with regimental uniform during summer, except for those officers in the Cavalry (121).

19 June 1834 – Military Generals and Field and Company-Grade Officers who on 4 March and 6 April of this year were prescribed War Ministry uniforms are ordered to have **shabracks** and pistol holders of the infantry pattern, dark green with red piping, with two rows of silver galloon and silver St.-Andrew's stars (Illus. 1020) (122).

22 July 1836 - Confirmation is given to a detailed regulation on the **uniform** prescribed on 4 March 1834 for officials in positions under the War Ministry. This regulation consists of articles with the following content:

1.) Officials in positions under the War Ministry are to wear a uniform of military cut, dark green with a red cloth collar and red piping down the fron and on the skirts; dark-green piping on the collar; dark-green cuffs and likewise dark-green cuff flaps, with red piping around the these cuffs and flaps; dark-green pants with red piping; boots with spurs.

2.) This uniform is to be used by:

a.) All officials in positions under the Provisioning and Commissariat Departments, or serving as Commissioners in these Departments; also, all officials of Intendance and Field Provisioning Bureaus.

b.) Officials in positions and institutions under the Artillery and Engineering administrations, but only if they are not officers commissioned in the Artillery or Corps of Engineers, and also officials in positions and institutions under the administration of the Department of Military Settlements, except for those officers commissioned in the Corps of Engineers of Military Settlements.

c.) Officials in Military Educational Institutions in a clerical, logistical, or police capacity, and also civilian officials on the Staffs of these Institutions or their Advisory Boards.

d.) Officials in Military Topography, in management of buildings used as quarters under the War Ministry, and civilian officials of the Military Topography Depot.

e.) Civilian officials on the Staffs of all forces in general and other military organizations, and also serving with regiments and various commands, who currently use uniforms of the previous pattern prescribed for the former Main Headquarters of HIS IMPERIAL MAJESTY and Ministry of War, except for bandmasters and music instruction officials, who have a special uniform established for them (see Chapter LXX below for a description of this uniform).

3.) The **buttons** on this uniform are hollow, silver, and have the following designs:

a.) Civilian officials on the Staffs of Guards forces or in Guards regiments have on their buttons the design prescribed for the Guards.

b.) Officials of all offices and agencies subordinate to War Ministry Departments, except for the Artillery Department, and on the Staffs of all other forces, Intendance Bureaus, Field Provisioning agencies, and those military administrative offices not mentioned below, have a single-flame grenade on the buttons.

c.) Officials in offices and agencies under the Artillery Department have on their buttons have a design made up of crossed cannons under a grenade.

d.) Officials of Military Educational Institutions and their Staffs and Advisory Boards have on their buttons an image of the state coat-of-arms with a semicircular radiance.

e.) Officials in regiments or various commands have on their buttons those designs prescribed for these regiments and commands by existing regulations.

4.) The **embroidery** on this uniform is silver and identical to that confirmed on 4 March 1834 for War Ministry Departments, but without edging.

5.) Military officials are to wear this uniform with the military appurtenances appropriate to the arm of service to which they belong. All wear the same straight silver buttonhole loops on the collar and cuff flaps. General-officer ranks wear this uniform in addition to the others they may use.

6.) In regard to **embroidery** on this uniform, civilian officials are divided into four categories:

A.) To the *first category* belong all the officials in the positions mentioned above in paragraph 2 whose duties rank them as class 5. In addition to the buttonhole loops on collar and cuff flaps they have a silver border, and on the cuffs just the border, according to the design currently used for general-officer ranks. On ceremonial days they are to wear white pants and jackboots with this uniform.

B.) To the *second category* belong those officials in classes 6 and 7. They have silver buttonhole loops on the collar and cuff flaps, without border or edging.

C.) To the *third category* belong those officials who through their duties in the Military administration are in the 8th, 9th, and 10th classes. They have two silver buttonhole loops only on the collar.

D.) To the *fourth category* belong those persons occupying positions rated as of the 12th or 14th classes, and who have officer ranks. They have no embroidery at all on the uniform.

7.) In addition to their prescribed uniform coat, officials of the first, second, and third categories also wear the 4th-category coat as an **undress uniform**.

8.) All officials, military as well as civilian, have a **frock coat** for everyday use, of the normal military style, dark green with a red cloth collar piped dark green, and with red piping on the cuffs and pockets, with the same silver buttons as on the dress coat.

9.) Official of temporary establishments created under military administration are to wear the uniform established for positions under the Ministry of War, based precisely on this Regulation.

10.) Officials in positions and establishments enumerated above in paragraphs 2 and 9 who are engaged in duties of high responsibility not addressed in the listings of classes and duties in the military administration are to use the War Ministry uniform with 1st-category embroidery as established on 4 March 1834 (123).

15 July 1837 - Military Generals and Field and Company-Grade Officers in the War Ministry and its subordinate offices are given a new-pattern **sash**, with narrow silver lace rather the previous wide, with three stripes of light-orange and black silk, and tied round with its whole width between the two lowest coat buttons (124).

17 December 1837 - These ranks are given **epaulettes** of a new pattern, with the addition of a fourth twist of thin cord (125).

2 January 1844 - These ranks are ordered to have a **cockade** on the front of the band of their forage caps, as established at this time for all branches and described in detail above for the uniforms of Grenadier regiments (126).

20 July 1849 - Field and Company-Grade Officers who wear the War Ministry uniform are ordered to have **helmets** with a Grenadier plate, without a number on the grenade. Those in the Cavalry are to have white plumes, and the rest—black (Illus. 1021) (127).

27 September 1849 - Generals in the War Ministry are ordered to have **helmets** of the pattern confirmed for Field and Company-Grade Officers of the Ministry, but with a gold IMPERIAL crown on the plate's shield and a white hair plume (128).

15 October 1849 - Infantry officers are given **half-sabers** in place of rapiers (129).

LXVII. OFFICIALS IN THE MEDICAL ADMINISTRATION. [*Chinovniki meditsinskoi chasti.*]

11 February 1826 – Instead of short pants with high boots, officials in the Medical administration are ordered to wear long dark-green **pants** with red piping, and short **boots** with driven-in **spurs**. For parade occasions, those in class 5 and higher keep their white cloth pants with jackboots and spurs (130).

26 July 1826 – These officials are ordered to have **coats** with nine (instead of six) buttons in front and, as before, red piping on the collar, cuffs, and tails (Illus. 1022 and 1023) (131).

26 July 1826 - Medical officials in infantry units, of the 5th class or higher, are ordered to have, during summer and on the same occasions as the officers of those units are prescribed to be in in summer (i.e. white linen) pants, the same **pants**, of a pattern like that of cloth pants (132).

However, the uniform distinctions between military medical officials remained the same as before, namely:

a.) For the Chief Inspector of the Army Medical Administration—silver buttonhole loops on the collar and cuffs, with tracery embroidered along the edges and a straight edging; on the pocket flaps only the embroidery and edging.

b.) For medical personnel of the 4th class and higher—the same as for the Chief Inspector but without embroidery on the pocket flaps.

c.) For the Field General-Staff-Doctor [*Polevoi General-Shtab-Doktor*], the Chief Doctor of the Army, Corps Staff-Doctors, and the Chief Doctors of 4th, 5th, and 6th class hospitals, who do not hold 4th-class rank—buttonhole loops and edging on the collar and cuffs, without embroidered tracery.

d.) For Chief Doctors in 1st, 2nd, and 3rd class hospitals, and regimental and other unit doctors holding the ranks of: Staff-Doctor, Doctor of Medicine and Surgery, Doctor of Medicine, or Medical Surgeon—silver buttonhole loops on collar and cuffs, without edging. *Note: Until 1834 the buttonhole loops for all medical officials of these four categories were somewhat crooked, but from that time they were sewn on straight, as on uniform coats in the War Ministry and its subordinate establishments.)*

e.) For medical personnel serving as Battalion Doctors, Interns [*Ordinatory*], and so on, who do not have the ranks of Staff-Doctor, Doctor of Medicine and Surgery, or Medical Surgeon, and also for physician's assistants of class 14 —coats without any embroidery at all. Medical personnel in Cavalry units do not have summer linen pants and carry the Cavalry rapier (133).

In 1835 Medical officials are given **shabracks** for those situations in which they had to be on horseback. These are of dark-green cloth with two rows of silver galloon, and having red piping on the edges (133).

4 July 1850 – Medical personnel with the forces of the **Separate Caucasus Corps** are allowed to wear uniforms of the patterns confirmed for this corps (134).

2 February 1852 – Instead of hats, Medical personnel in the Army are ordered to wear infantry **helmets** without plumes, with silver mountings. Those in Guards forces or under Military Educational Institutions are to have the Guards helmet plate (Illus. 1024), while the rest are to have the Army pattern with a blank shield. Medical personnel of the rank of Actual State Counselor or higher have a general officer's plate. The replacement of the hat with the helmet also applies to physicians of the St.-Petersburg Medical-Surgical Academy and the War Ministry's Medical Department, who have the uniform prescribed for doctors with the forces. Along with this change, all the Medical personnel identified here are ordered to have **cockades** on the band of the forage cap (135).

2 March 1852 – It is ordered that:

1.) Personal Physicians, Honorary Personal Physicians, Personal Surgeons, and Honorary Personal Surgeons at HIS IMPERIAL MAJESTY'S Court, if from the military medical administration, are to have: a.) the Guards plate on the **helmet**, with a monogram of HIS MAJESTY'S Name, similar to the helmets of Generals in HIS MAJESTY'S Suite, and b.) on the coat's shoulders—straps of silver general officer's cord.

2.) This style of **shoulder strap** on the coat is prescribed for Medical personnel occupying the positions listed below, if they hold a rank no lower than Actual State Counselor:

Chief Inspector of the Army Medical Administration.

General-Staff-Doctor of the Active Army, Chief Staff-Doctor of the Guards Corps, Staff-Doctor of the Separate Caucasus Corps, Chief Doctor of Military Educational Institutions.

Staff-Doctor of Army and Separate corps.

Staff-Doctor of the troops located in Finland.

Staff-Doctor of the Guards Infantry Corps and the Guards Reserve Cavalry Corps.

Senior Doctors of the forces on the Caucasian Line and on the Black Sea littoral, Instructional Carabinier regiments, and military cantonist establishments.

Assistant General-Staff-Doctor of the Active Army.

Chief Doctors of 3rd, 4th, 5th, and 6th class hospitals.

Inspectors of Military Medical Administrations for the Don and Black Sea, and Members of the Military Medical Academic Committee (136).

28 May 1852 – Students of the Medical-Surgical Academy, instead of hats, are ordered to wear **helmets** without plumes, of the military medical pattern, without an officer's cockade, and with a white metal Army plate on the shield of which are the cut-out letters M. X. A. (Illus. 1025). All metallic mountings on the helmet are bright and not matte (137).

29 April 1854 – Medical personnel with the forces during wartime are ordered to wear campaign **greatcoats** of the pattern confirmed at this time for infantry officers who are mounted when in unit formation, but the button prescribed for them are white and smooth, while the collar and shoulder straps are dark green with red piping, with silver galloon on the strapes, sewn across in a diagonal direction (Illus. 1026) (138).

1 May 1854 – Medical personnel at hospitals in the **Caucasus** are prescribed uniform clothing of the kind for Medical personnel with the Caucasus Corps' combatant forces (139).

11 October 1854 – It is ordered that:

1.) Medical personnel in the military are to wear **shoulder straps** on dress coats and frocks according to the confirmed patterns: for field-grade officer equivalent ranks—of smooth silver fabric [*serebryanaya tkan' nepletenaya*] (Illus. 1027), and for physicians' assistants [*lekarskie pomoshchniki*] promoted from medic [*fel'dsher*] to the 14th class—of dark-green cloth.

2.) Military Medical personnel of general-officer rank are to keep their previously established shoulder straps of plaited silver cord [*serebryanaya vitaya kanitel'*] (140).

Note 1: **Pharmaceutical officials** [*chinovniki Farmatsevticheskoi chasti*] have the same uniforms as prescribed for Battalion Doctors and Interns, i.e. without silver embroidery on the collar and cuffs (141).

Note 2: **Veterinary officials** [*chinovniki Veterinarnoi chasti*] have uniforms and shabracks similar to those for medical personnel but, as before, of dark-blue color, with such distinctions so that *Senior Veterinary Doctors* are prescribed two buttonhole loops on collar and cuffs, *Junior Veterinary Doctors*—two buttonhole loops on the cuffs and one on the collar, and *Veterinary Assistants of the 1st Grade* [*Veterinarnye Pomoshchniki 1-go Otdeleniya*] have no loops at all. All these ranks are prescribed Cavalry rapiers (Illus. 1028) (142).

LXVIII. QUARTERMASTERS IN THE GUARDS CORPS. [*Kvartirmistry Gvardeiskago korpusa.*]

11 February 1826 – Instead of their previous double-breasted coats and pants with high boots, Guards Corps quartermasters are ordered to have a single-breasted **coat** with nine buttons in front, red piping added along the front opening and from the bottom front to the coattails; long dark-green **pants** with red piping on the side seams, and short **boots** with driven-in spurs (Illus. 1029) (143).

26 July 1826 - Quartermasters of Guards infantry units are ordered, during summer at those times when the officers of these units are prescribed to be in summer (i.e. white linen) **pants**, to have the same, of the same pattern as for cloth pants (144).

Guards Corps quartermasters are also prescribed **shabracks** of dark-green cloth, with two rows of silver galloon and red cloth piping on the edges (145).

2 February 1852 - Guards Corps quartermasters are ordered to have infantry **helmets**, without plumes, and with a silvered Guards plate, and to have a **cockade** on the band of the forage cap (146).

29 April 1854 - Quartermasters are ordered to have, during wartime, campaign greatcoats like those prescribed for Medical personnel, but without piping on the shoulder straps (147).

LXIX. AUDITORS. [*Auditory.*]

Auditors [military legal advisors - M. C.] are prescribed the same **uniform clothing** as the preceding, with the difference that the Field Auditor-General [*Polevoi General-Auditor*] and those Senior Auditors [*Ober-Auditory*] who held rank in classes IV or V have the uniform established for 1st category ranks in positions under the War Ministry (148).

2 February 1852 - In place of hats, auditors are ordered to wear infantry **helmets**, without plumes, and with white mountings. Those in Guards forces or under the administration of Military Educational Institutions have the Guards helmet plate, while all others have the Army pattern, with a blank shield. Along with this they are given **cockades** for the band of the forage cap (149).

LXX. RIDING MASTERS. [*Bereitory.*]

Riding masters, who keep the same uniform as for Quartermasters in the Guards Corps but without cuff flaps and with two buttons on the cuffs, from **1826** have long dark-green **pants** with red piping (Illus. 1030), and from **1828 riding trousers** (grey) with only a single line of red piping and no stripes. They carry cavalry **rapiers**. Those in the Riding Masters School, instead of dark-green pants, have dark-green *chakchiry* **pants** with a red stripe, and grey riding trousers with red piping (Illus. 1031). All Riding Masters are allowed to wear **moustaches** (150).

27 November 1827 - A new regulation for the **Guards Riding Masters School** is confirmed with the following description of the uniforms for its personnel:

1.) If the School Commander is from the Guards, then he keeps the uniform of the regiment to which he belongs; if he is from the Army, he wears the uniform of an officer at large in the Cavalry.

2.) The School Police Chief is prescribed a uniform of the pattern for War Ministry officials.

3.) The Chief Riding Master [*Ober-Bereitor*] has gold buttonhole loops on his coat's collar and cuffs, with a border and edging [*s bordurom i kantom*], and on the shoulders, as a kind of shoulder strap, plaited gold cord [*perevitye zolotye kanitel'nye snurki*] (Illus. 1032, 1033, and 1034).

4.) Senior Riding Masters have gold buttonhole loops on collar and cuffs, with edging and a border (Illus. 1035).

5.) Junior Riding Masters wear on collar and cuffs gold edging with a border.

6.) The Head Riding Master as well as Riding Masters are prescribed a three-cornered hat with a black plume, sabers, instead of *chakchiry* pants—riding trousers of grey-blue cloth, and buttons with a design.

7.) Students in the Guards Riding Master School have helmets of the pattern for Cavalry Cadets [*yunkery*] in the School for Guards Officer Candidates, with red brass mountings and black hair plumes. *Sabers* of the old Guards Horse Artillery pattern, on a deerskin sword belt. Single-breasted *coat* of dark-green cloth, with a collar of the same, red shoulder straps, red piping on the collar, front opening, and cuffs; Guards buttons. *Riding trousers* of grey-blue Guards cloth, with red trim (Illus. 1037). *Greatcoat* of grey Guards cloth, with a dark-green collar, red shoulder straps, and red piping on the collar. In addition, for riding in the manège they have: single-breasted *jacket* of dark-green cloth with collar and cuffs of the same, piped red. With the jacket are worn: grey-blue *riding trousers* of Guards cloth, with red piping; *forage cap* of dark-green Guards cloth, with red piping; chamois *gloves*, without gauntlet cuffs (151).

17 March 1851 – HIGHEST Authority orders that:

1.) The **shoulder straps** of gold general-officer's cord prescribed for the Guards Riding Masters School's Head Riding Master is abollished, leaving him to wear these upon reaching class 5 rank.

2.) In place of the tricorn hat with black plume, the Head Riding Master and Senior and Junior Riding Masters are prescribed **helmets** with black hair plumes, of the pattern for School students (Illus. 1038). **Students**, instead of chamois sword belts, are to have these of red morocco, with a sword knot of the same; shoulder straps on the coat and greatcoat—of dark-green cloth instead of red, with red piping and the cut-out Cyrillic letters B. Sh. backed by yellow cloth (Illus. 1039); red edging to the band and top of the forage cap (152).

2 February 1852 - Riding Masters with the forces and under military administration are to have, instead of hats, infantry **helmets**, without plumes, with white mountings. Those with Guards troops or under the administration of the Military Education Institutions have a Guards helmet plate, while the rest have the Army pattern with a blank shield. Riding Masters not holding a classed rank and carrying out their duties by private contract are to wear helmets and forage caps without a cockade (153).

29 April 1854 - Riding Masters are ordered to have, during wartime, campaign greatcoats of the pattern prescribed at this same time for Medical personnel, but without piping on the shoulder straps (154).

LXXI. BANDMASTERS AND MUSIC INSTRUCTION OFFICIALS. [*Kapel'neistery i chinovniki dlya obucheniya muzyki.*]

From **1826** these persons have uniforms of the same color and pattern as prescribed for Battalion Doctors, Interns, and Physicians' Assistants, but with gold buttons instead of silver, and this comprises their *undress uniform*. For their *parade coat* Band Masters in the Guards have gold embroidered buttonhole loops and edging, while in the Army they only have the loops and no edging (Illus. 1040). Those with infantry troops wear infantry swords, while those with the cavalry have cavalry rapiers. Both are prescribed shabracks with pistol holders, of dark-green cloth, two rows of gold galloon, and red cloth piping around the edges (155).

2 February 1852 - These persons are given **helmets** in place of hats, but without plumes, with yellow mountings. Those with Guards troops or in Military Educational Institutions have a Guards helmet plate, and the rest have the Army pattern, with a blank shield. Those not holding classed rank but rather carrying out their duties by contract are not to have a cockade on the helmet or forage cap (156).

LXXII. ARSENAL INSPECTORS. [*Tseikhvartery.*]

11 February 1826 - Arsenal Inspectors [*Tseikhvartery* - from the German *Zeugwärter* - M.C.] of Artillery and Engineer establishments, instead of their previous double-breasted coats and pants with high boots, are ordered to have single-breasted **coats** with nine buttons in front, with red piping added down the front and from the front to the tails, and on the cuff flaps; long dark-green **pants** with red piping on the side seams, and short **boots** without spurs (Illus. 1041) (157).

2 February 1852 - These personnel are ordered to have infantry **helmets** without a plume, with white mountings and an Army plate with a blank shield. A **cockade** is added to the forage cap (158).

LXXIII. CIVILIAN TEACHING OFFICIALS IN MILITARY EDUCATIONAL INSTITUTIONS.
[*Grazhdanskie chinovniki uchebnoi chasti Voenno-Uchebnykh zavedenii.*]

6 August and 3 December 1826 – *Professors [professory]* in Military Educational Institutions, serving on their staffs, on parade occasions are ordered to wear a single-breasted **coat** of the prescribed pattern for civilian officials, of dark-blue cloth, with gold embroidery and edging (according to the design used in the Warsaw Applied School [*Varshavskaya Applikatsionnaya shkola*] and Kalisz Cadet Corps) on a red cloth collar and cuffs, with red piping down the front, from the front to the tails, and on the pockets; with flat gilt buttons on which is the image of a two-headed Russian eagle over a stand of arms. Dark-blue cloth **pants** are prescribed to be worn with this coat, without piping; officers' hats and infantry officers' rapiers, with a silver sword knot (Illus. 1042 and 1043). *Instructors [uchiteli]* holding classed ranks are prescribed the same uniform but without the gold embroidered edging on collar and cuffs (Illus. 1043), and for *instructors not holding classed rank* are established dark-blue *undress coats* (of the pattern for standard frock coats), with the same buttons as on the coats of professors and instructors who hold classed rank; dark-blue vests or gilets with the same buttons as on the undress coat but of smaller size; dark-blue pants and round hats. The exactly same undress coats are given to professors and instructors for everyday use (159).

27 May 1836 - Civilian officials on the instructional staffs of Military Educational Institutions are ordered to have the **uniform** prescribed in 1827 for professors and instructors, but with the addition of red piping on the pants and the red cloth collar and cuffs changed to dark-blue velvet, with the following distinctions:

a.) For class Inspectors [*Inspektory klassov*]—collar and cuffs with edging and embroidery a little less than established in 1827 (Illus. 1044, 1045, and 1046).

b.) For assistants to class Inspectors and for Teacher Examiners [*Nastavniki-Nablyudateli*]—collar with embroidery and edging, but cuffs with just edging and no embroidery.

c.) For Instructors of sciences and languages—collar and cuffs without embroidery, with double edging.

d.) For Instructors of arts, Tutors, Librarians, and Museum and Collections Curators—collar without embroidery, with double edging, but cuffs without embroidery or edging and only with red piping and two buttons instead of the three prescribed for the preceding officials.

e.) For assistants to fencing and gymnastics Instructors, holding classed ranks—collar and cuffs without embroidery or edging, with just red piping.

For all these ranks **buttons** are flat with the image prescribed for Military Educational Institutions, i.e. the state coat-of-arms with a semicircular radiance (Illus. 1045).

All these persons keep the dark-blue **undress coats** of civilian cut, with the same buttons as on the dress coat and with a dark-blue collar: velvet for those of classed rank and of cloth for those without rank. The first are further distinguished from the latter by having three buttons on each pocket, which is not prescribed for those not holding classed rank (160).

20 December 1840 - The dark-blue color of coats, collars, cuffs, and pants of the ranks mentioned in the preceding paragraph is changed to **dark green**, keeping the rank differences as before (Illus. 1047, 1048, and 1049) (161).

LXXIV. MILITARY CANTONISTS, WITH THE MILITARY INSTRUCTORS INSTITUTE AND AUDITORS SCHOOL.
[*Voennye kantonisty, s Voenno-Uchitel'skim Institutom i Auditorskoyu Shkoloyu.*]

a.) *Military cantonists in battalions, half-battalions, and separate companies.*

26 November 1826 - With the transformation of the St.-Petersburg Military Orphans Section to the St.-Petersburg Military Cantonist Battalion, with its reorganization into four militarily structured and ranked [*ranzhirovannyi*] companies and one unstructured, the military cantonists in it keep their previous grey **uniform** with yellow shoulder straps, and the following is ordered in regard to other parts of the coat:

a.) For the 1st Company (cantonists being trained as teachers and topographers)—black collar and cuffs with red piping; black cuff flaps without piping; white buttons (Illus. 1050).

b.) For the 2nd Company (Artillery cantonists)—black collar and cuffs with red piping; red cuff flaps; yellow buttons (Illus. 1051).

c.) For the 3rd Company (Engineer cantonists)—black collar and cuffs with red piping; red cuff flaps; white buttons (Illus. 1051).

d.) For the 4th (cantonists from the Army and Garrison administrations) and 5th Companies (younger age cantonists from all the mentioned categories), as before—yellow collar and cuffs, grey cuff flaps, white buttons (Illus. 1052).

In all companies the band of the **forage cap** is the same color as the collar, and **jackets** are single breasted (162).

19 November 1831 - In all battalions, half-battalions, and companies of military cantonists jackets, winter trousers, and forage caps are ordered to be **dark-green** instead of grey, with the same collar, cuffs, cuff flaps, and shoulder straps. On the shoulder straps, however, are red piping and the cut-out battalion number backed with red cloth, following the numerical order in the general list of all battalions, half-battalions, and separate companies of military cantonists (Illus. 1053). The bands on forage caps and collars and shoulder straps on greatcoats are also to be dark green, with the shoulder straps prescribed to the be same as on the jacket. In the 2nd and 3rd (Artillery and Engineer) Companies of the St.-Petersburg Battalion are left, as before, black collars and cuffs with red piping, red cuff flaps, and the previous buttons: yellow in the 2nd Company and white in the 3rd. —*Teachers* of non-commissioned officer rank are prescribed the uniform for non-commissioned officers of Mobile Invalid companies, but with the cut-out battalion number of the shako grenade and red piping and numbers on shoulder straps (Illus. 1054). Teachers in the St.-Petersburg Battalion are prescribed additional red piping on the collar, cuffs, and cuff flaps (163).

20 February 1833 - The previous summer pants of teachers of non-commissioned officer rank, with buttons below and integral spats, are replaced with the same **pants** that are introduced at this time for all infantry troops (164).

10 July 1835 - In order to distinguish **lance-corporals** [*yefreitory*] from other cantonists, they are given tape to be sewn across the jacket's shoulder straps, of yellow lace, placed 1/2 vershok [7/8 inch] from the shoulder seam (165).

8 November 1836 - With the division of the **Voronezh Battalion** into two and its designation to provide non-commissioned officers for the regiments of the 3rd Reserve Cavalry Corps (1st and 2nd Dragoon Divisions), and fireworkers for the Artillery of this corps, the military cantonists of the structured companies and batteries of these battalions are ordered to have collars, shoulder straps, and buttons of the color and patterns of the regiments and batteries which they are assigned to support, in the same way as for cantonist squadrons and batteries in Cavalry Military Settlement Districts, described below (166).

July 1845 – In place of shakos, non-commissioned officer teachers in all battalions, half-battalions, and companies are given **helmets** identical to those introduced in 1844 for all infantry troops, and with the same grenade as was on the shako (Illus. 1055) (167).

19 May 1847 - Teachers of non-commissioned officer rank and cantonists are ordered to have dark-green **forage caps** with a band of the same color, without piping. On the band is cut out and backed by yellow cloth: No. of the company and the Cyrillic letter R. (168).

22 June 1848 - Lower ranks instructing formations and invalids are allowed to wear **moustaches** (169).

10 January 1852 - In military cantonist battalions **forage caps** are introduced to replace helmets, of dark-green cloth, with a visor and chinstrap, and designated for use in those situations when the helmet had previously been worn (170).

b.) *Military Instructors Institute.*

8 September 1827 - Teachers assigned to the founding of the Military Instructors Institute [*Voenno-Uchitel'skii Institut*] at the St.-Petersburg Military Cantonists Battalion are ordered to have the same uniforms as given on 1 November 1831 to all military cantonists, except for the addition of red piping on the collar, cuffs, cuff flaps, and forage cap, with red shoulder straps and yellow buttons. However, since the establishment of the institute was never carried through, the uniforms for it were likewise never made (171).

c.) *Auditors School.*

26 March 1832 - Pupils at the *Auditors School*, established on this date at the St.-Petersburg Battalion of Military Cantonists, are ordered to have standard cantonist uniforms, with the addition of silver galloon on the collar, and with the shoulder straps prescribed for Instructional Carabinier regiments but without a number (Illus. 1056) (172).

11 September 1846 - A new administrative regulation is confirmed for the *War Ministry Auditors School*, by which:

1.) The Director and Field and Company-Grade officers of the School, being in the Army at large, wear the War Ministry uniform.

2.) Students at the School have the standard cantonist uniform with the addition, as before, of silver galloon on the collar, and of shoulder straps as for Instructional Carabinier regiments (173).

8 November 1854 - Students of the Auditors School's 1st Class selected to be section lance-corporals [*otdelennye yefreitory*] are ordered to have, as rank distinction, silver galloon sewn along the center of the shoulder straps on jackets and greatcoats (174).

d.) *The Young Noble Boys Section of the Novgorod Military Cantonist Battalion.*

29 December 1834 - Pupils in the Young Noble Boys section [*Maloletnoe Dvoryanskoe otdelenie*] of the Novgorod Military Cantonist Battalion, established on this date, are ordered to have standard cantonist uniforms with such improvements in quality as the funding of the institution may allow, and with a red collar on jackets and greatcoats, following the example of Cadet corps (Illus. 1057) (175). Note: In 1844 this section was formed into unstructured companies of the Novgorod and Polotsk Cadet Corps, as mentioned above in the chapter on Military Educational Institutions.

d.) *Military cantonists in Cavalry squadrons and Artillery batteries of Cavalry Military Settlements.*

8 August 1836 - On this date in the Cavalry Districts of Military Settlements two squadrons are established for each regiment of the 1st and 2nd Reserve Cavalry Corps and 5th Light Cavalry Division, as well as five batteries for the Artillery of these forces. The military cantonists of these squadrons and batteries are ordered to have standard cantonist uniforms as prescribed for the battalions, half-battalions, and separate companies of military cantonists. In the squadrons for Cuirassier regiments and in the Artillery batteries—of dark-green cloth, and in the squadrons for Lancer and Hussar regiments—of dark-blue; for all the collars, cuffs, piping, shoulder straps, and buttons are of the colors and patterns of those regiments and batteries to which the aforesaid cantonists belong (Illus. 1058). They are not prescribed any weapons, but for training they use wooden sabers, pikes, and guns (176).

e.) *Military cantonists at Powder Works, Arms Factories, and Arsenals.*

Uniforms are the same as in military cantonist battalions, but with shoulder straps as for lower ranks in the referenced works and arsenals (177).

19 May 1847 - Dark-green forage caps are confirmed for these cantonists, with the same color band, on which there are cut-out letters on yellow cloth designating the place to which they belong (178).

f.) *Military cantonists in Guards forces.*

8 October 1832 - Cantonists in the schools at all Infantry and Cavalry regiments of the Guards Corps, and at the Guards Sapper Battalion, Guards Équipage, and Guards Artillery brigades, as well as at the Guards Invalid companies' Headquarters, are ordered to have: *jackets*—for the Infantry of the same color as the dress coat, but in the Cavalry the color of the stable jacket [*leibik*], with collar, shoulder straps, and buttons as prescribed in the Infantry for greatcoats, but as for lower combatant ranks' stable jackets in the Cavalry; *pants* (in the Infantry) as for combatant ranks, *riding trousers* (in the Cavalry) of grey-blue cloth, without leather reinforcement, and with the piping prescribed for the regiment; **forage caps** as for combatant ranks, but without piping around the top and without a number or letter on the band (Illus. 1059); *greatcoats* as for these same ranks (179).

g.) *Cantonists at Military Educational Institutions.*

11 April 1831 - For cantonists at the Corps of Pages, several Cadet Corps, and Nobiliary Regiment, from the age of seven, **jackets** and other clothing are ordered to be made from the time-expired worn student uniforms of these establishments, in all respects conforming to the last named one, except for collars, which for cantonists are prescribed to be dark green with red piping and, on each side, a red tab. They have no piping around the top of the forage cap, nor numbers or letters on the band (Illus. 1060) (180).

14 July 1853 - **Pants** are ordered to be made for the cantonists, of dark-green cloth with red piping, and on **forage caps** there are to be cut-outs according to the establishment (181)

LXXV. OFFICERS OF MILITARY CANTONIST BATTALIONS, HALF-BATTALIONS, AND SEPARATE COMPANIES.

[*Ofitsery batalionov, polubatalionov i otdel'nykh rot voennykh kantonistov.*]

These officers are prescribed the uniform for officers at large in the Army, with the addition of the battalion's, half-battalion's, or company's brigade number embroidered in silver cord on the field of the epaulette (182).

LXXVI. LOWER NONCOMBATANT RANKS OF HIS IMPERIAL MAJESTY'S MAIN HEADQUARTERS, THE MINISTRY OF WAR, AND ORGANIZATIONS SUBORDINATE TO THIS MINISTRY.

[*Nizhnie nestroevye chiny Glavnago Shtaba EGO IMPERATORSKAGO VELICHESTVA, Voennago Ministerstva i mest, semu Ministerstvu podvedomstvennykh.*]

26 July 1826 - For clerks and office workers [*pisarya i sluzhiteli*] at HIS IMPERIAL MAJESTY'S Main Headquarters, Military Topography Depot, and Ministry of War the stripes on **pants** are removed, leaving only a single line of red piping on the side seams (Illus. 1061) (in the first the clerks and workers have **frock coats** with red piping on the collar and cuffs, and red cuff flaps; in the second frock coats with light-blue [*svetlosinii*] piping on the collar and cuffs, and light-blue cuff flaps; and in the last with red piping on the collar and on slit cuffs without flaps). Since this year these persons are ordered to wear, in summertime, white linen pants. Uniforms similar to those for War Ministry clerks are also given to **hospital attendants** [*gospital'nye fel'dshera*], as before without shoulder straps, with white buttons instead of yellow, silver galloon instead of gold, and dark-green lining instead of red (Illus. 1061) (183).

In 1832, with the transfer of Departments and other parts of HIS IMPERIAL MAJESTY'S Main Headquarters to the War Ministry, all clerks already in the War Ministry are given red flaps to the **cuffs**, as until now was only for clerks in the Main Headquarters (184).

5 May 1844 - War Ministry clerks are ordered to have cut-out Cyrillic **letters** on frock-coat shoulder straps and forage-cap bands, backed by yellow cloth, according to the following list (Illus. 1062):

a.) General Staff Department—G.Sh.

b.) Inspection Department—I.

c.) Artillery Department and its subordinate offices—A.

d.) Commissariat Department and its subordinate offices, hospitals, and clinics—K.

e.) Provisioning Department and its subordinate offices—P.

f.) Department of Military Settlements and its subordinate offices—V.P.

g.) Medical Department and its subordinate offices—M.

h) Auditors Department and in general all clerks in offices subordinate to this Department—A.

i.) War Ministry Chancellery—K. M.

j.) Military Academic Committee—U.K. (*Uchen. Komit.*)

k.) Committee established by HIGHEST Authority on 18 August 1814—K. R. (*Kom. Ranen.* [*Committee for Wounded*])

l.) Administration of IMPERIAL Military Stud Establishments—K. Z. (*Konsk. Zaved.*)

m.) Military Academy—V. A.

Based on this directive clerks at the Headquarters of Military Educational Institutions are prescribed the letters—U.Z. (185).

21 January 1846 - Guards and workers of the Commissariat and Provisioning administrations, instead of shakos, are ordered to have **forage caps** with visors and chinstraps, and instead of tailcoats and pants—frock coats and *sharavary* pants (Illus. 1063) (186).

15 May 1846 - Confirmation is given to a new organizational table for the Guards Cavalry Remount Commission with prescribed uniforms for lower ranks of the remount command, according to which they are to have: cossack coat [*kazakin*] of dark-green cloth with red piping on the collar and cuffs; *sharavary pants* of dark-green cloth with red trim; *greatcoat* of grey cloth with a dark-green collar with a red buttonhole loop and red piping; *forage cap* of dark-green cloth with red piping on the band (187).

19 May 1847 - Particulars of **forage caps** are confirmed:

1.) For clerks in War Ministry Departments and Agencies, and subordinate offices: dark-green forage cap with visor; dark-green band with one line of red piping around the top edge, with cut-out Cyrillic letters on yellow cloth, according to Department: General Staff—G.Sh., Inspection—I., Auditors—A., Commissariat—K., Provisioning—P., Military Settlements—V.P., Medical—M., War Ministry Chancellery—K.M., HIS IMPERIAL MAJESTY'S Military Campaign Chancellery—V.P.K., Committee established by HIGHEST Authority on 18 August 1814—K. R., Administration of Military Stud Establishments—K.Z., Military Academy—V.A., Military Academic Committee—U.K., and the Chesmene Charity Shelter—Ch.B. With a black *band* with red piping around both edges, and letters according to Department: Artillery—A., Engineer—I.; according to headquarters: the Master-General of Ordnance's [*General-Fel'dtseikhmeister*]—G.F., and of the Inspector-General for Engineering—G.I. For all the above there is red piping around the top of the forage cap.

2.) The cap for draftsmen, typographers, accountants, watchmen, and craftsmen under the War Ministry and other agencies is similar to that prescribed for clerks at these places.

3.) For engravers, inscribers, mechanics, and craftsmen of the Mechanical works and Topography Depo, under the General Staff Department: dark-green *forage cap* with visor; dark-green *band* with one blue [*svetlosinii*] piping around the top edge; and with cut-out letters on yellow cloth, as for clerks at the General Staff; blue *piping* around the top of cap

4.) For keepers and workers under the Commissariat and Provisioning administrations: dark-green *cap* [*shapka*] with visor and chinstrap; dark-green *band* with red piping around the top edge, and with cut-out Cyrillic letters backed by yellow cloth: in the Commissariat—K., in Provisioning—P.; no piping around the top.

5.) For hospital orderlies, apprentice and student apothecaries in local hospitals, as well as auditors' assistants and clerks in: the administrative offices of Military Governors, Commandants, Military Courts [*Ordonans-gauzy*], Corps and Regional Chiefs of the Internal Guard, the Corps of Gendarmes, and other internal agencies: dark-green *forage cap*, with visor; dark-green *band* with a single piping around the top edge; red *piping* around the top of the forage cap.

6.) For conductors in Artillery, Engineer, and Military Settlements administrations—dark-green *forage cap* without a visor; black *band* with two lines of piping, around both edges, and with cut-out letters, as for clerks of these Departments; red *piping* around the top of the forage cap.

7.) For craftsmen in Telegraph companies: grey *forage cap* with visor and chinstrap; grey *band* without piping, with the company No. and the letter T. cut out and backed by yellow cloth; without piping around the top of the cap.

8.) For military-labor battalions and companies under the Department of Military Settlements: dark-green *forage cap*; *band* with two light-green lines of piping around the edges, and with the company No. and Cyrillic letter R. cut out and backed with yellow cloth; light-green *piping* around the top of the forage cap (188).

2 December 1849 - Lower ranks at the Headquarters of the Inspector of All Artillery and the Inspector of Engineering are ordered to have, for the first—Cyrillic I. A., and for the second—I. I., on the **shoulder straps** of their greatcoats and frock coats and on the band of the **forage cap**, in place of the previous letters (Illus. 1064) (189).

LXXVII. LOWER NONCOMBATANT RANKS AT MILITARY EDUCATIONAL INSTITUTIONS.
[*Nizhnie nestroevye chiny Voenno-Uchebnykh zavedenii.*]

From 1826, clerks and workers at the various Cadet corps and Nobiliary Regiment are prescribed the same **uniform clothing** as for clerks and workers under the Ministry of War, but for all of them with collars, cuff flaps, and shoulder straps of the colors particular to the establishment. Those of non-commissioned officer rank also have cadet pattern galloon. **Forage caps** are dark green for all, with a visor, red band, and dark-green piping around the top (Illus. 1065) (190).

Those lower ranks in the service companies [*sluzhitel'skiya roty*] of Military Educational institutions who came from the Guards have, since 23 July 1836, **Guards buttonhole loops** on the frock coat's collar and cuff flaps, of yellow tape [*bason*] with red stripes (Illus. 1066) (191). Room servants [*komnatnnye sluzhiteli*] at the Artillery and Main Engineering Schools, Corps of Pages, and School for Guards Officer Candidates are prescribed uniforms similar to those for officers' orderlies at these institutions (192).

19 May 1847 - **Forage caps** are confirmed as:

1.) For supply sergeants [*kaptenarmusy*], musicians, drummers, and hornists at Cadet corps—the same as for students.

2.) For other lower ranks: dark-green forage caps with a visor; band with the cut-out letters of the institution, backed by yellow cloth; dark-green *piping* around the top of the forage cap.

3.) For clerks at the Headquarters of Military Educational Institutions—dark-green *forage cap* with visor; dark-green *band* with red piping around the top edge and with the cut-out Cyrillic letters U. Z. on yellow cloth; red *piping* around the top of the cap.

4.) For hospital orderlies and apprentice and student apothecaries at local hospitals, as well as auditors' assistants—dark-green *forage cap* with visor; dark-green *band* with red piping around the top edge; red *piping* around the top of the forage cap (193).

8 June 1853 - The following changes are prescribed for the **uniforms** of lower ranks in Military Educational institutions:

1.) Musicians, drummers, and hornists are to have the uniform currently used in the 1st Cadet Corps, adapted to various institution's particuular distinctions. Drummers at the Main Engineering and Michael Artillery Schools are to insert red piping into the collar seam and not cover it with the musician's tape sewn around the bottom of the collar.

2.) Supply sergeants are not to trim cuff flaps with galloon, and they as well as all lower ranks of non-commissioned officer status (except musicians, drummers, and hornists) are to have the galloon of the 2nd Guards Division instead of Cadet galloon.

3.) Clerks at the Michael Artillery School are to have their frock coats and pants made from Guards cloth, dark green for the coats and grey for the pants.

4.) Student riding masters at the 1st and 2nd Cadet Corps are to trim their pants with leather and have straps passing under the boot; they are to be issued chamois gloves and spurs.

5.) Clerks and lower ranks in service companies are to have dark-green cloth cuff flaps on the frock coat, with red piping.

6.) Hospital orderlies are to have uniforms identical to those for clerks, except that flaps are not sewn down on the cuffs, but fastened by two small hooks.

7.) Lower ranks in service companies are to have buttons with eagles.

8.) Workers at the Corps of Pages and Main Engineering and Michael Artillery Schools are henceforth to have frock coats made instead of dress coats, of dark-green Guards cloth, while pants are to be of grey. Volontarily hired servants at the Corps of Pages and School for Guards Officer Candidates are to have coats and pants of dark-green Guards cloth, of the style for orderlies; greatcoats and forage caps are also as for orderlies.

9.) Greatcoats for lower ranks at the Main Engineering and Michael Artillery Schools are to be made from grey soldier cloth.

10.) Workers at the Corps of Pages and clerks and watchmen at the Michael Artillery School are to have forage caps with visors.

11.) Clerks, hospital orderlies, and watchmen at the Main Engineering and Michael Artillery Schools are to have cut-out Cyrillic letters on the forage-cap band: in the Main Engineering School—G. I., and in the Michael Artillery School—M. A.

12.) Forage caps for all lower ranks throughout Military Educational institutions are to be made with a quilted canvas lining.

13.) Collars and shoulder straps for clerks in the Corps of Pages are to be made with green piping, and pants with red (194).

LXXVIII. OFFICERS OF SERVICE COMPANIES AT MILITARY EDUCATIONAL INSTITUTIONS.
[*Ofitsery sluzhitel'skikh rot Voenno-Uchebnykh zavedenii.*]

These officers have the same uniforms as for officers of Mobile Invalid companies and Invalid commands, but with the numbers and letters particular to the institution's service company embroidered on the field of the epaulette with silver cord (195).

LXXIX. ORDERLIES. [*Denshchiki.*]

11 February 1826 – With their previous uniform, all orderlies are ordered to have grey **riding trousers**: without stripes for infantry forces, and with stripes for cavalry (196).

Based on regulations confirmed by HIGHEST Authority on 15 January 1802, they wear the same **pants** and **boots** as prescribed for the person whom they serve (Illus. 1067).

3 October 1848 - HIGHEST Authority orders that: officers' orderlies in the **Separate Caucasus Corps** are to have half-caftans with *sharavary* pants of the patterns prescribed for officers, with covered cloth buttons. They are allowed to wear out the previous coats with pants until such time as officers find it possible to have new-pattern clothing made for them. Forage caps and greatcoats for orderlies keep the patterns now in use (197).

31 October 1852- HIGHEST Authority orders that:

1.) Orderlies of Generals and Field and Company-Grade officers are to have leather **helmets** instead of hats (Illus. 1068).

2.) Helmets are to be worn only in those situations when previously hats were used.

3.) The pattern for these helmets is the same as for lower ranks but with the following differences:

a.) The top brass part is to be a ball without flames.

b.) The plate is to have no monogram or numbers, nor any honor scroll.

4.) Fittings to the helmet are white or yellow according to the helmet of the officer whom the orderly attends; tombak in the Guards and Military Educational Institutions, brass in the Army, and tin for those prescribed white metal. The fittings are to be neither gilded nor silvered.

5.) Helmets in the Cavalry, Horse Artillery, and Horse-Pioneer double-squadrons are to have a metal edge on the front visor , and in Cuirasssier regiments and the Corps of Gendarmes—metal side strips, as on officers' helmets (Illus. 1068).

6.) Plates are to be exactly the same as those on the helmets of the officers on whom the orderlies attend, except with *embossed [vy-bivnye]* stars where prescribed, and never any monograms, numbers or honor scrolls.

7.) Orderlies to officers in the Separate Caucasus Corps have *papakhi* fleece headdresses without galloon, piping, or honor scrolls.

8.) In the Caucasian Mountaineer Half-Squadron and in the commands under HIS IMPERIAL MAJESTY'S Own Escort, orderlies have *shapka* headdresses of officer pattern but without galloon (198).

22 December 1852 - The following description of orderlies' **uniforms** is confirmed by HIGHEST Authority:

a.) *Forage cap*—in all branches of the same pattern and color as for officers, without a visor, and with piping on the top and sides in the same colors for officers.

b.) *Tailcoat*—of dark-blue cloth in the L.-Gd. Horse and all Lancer regiments (Illus. 1068), light blue for Gendarmes, grey for the Train, and of dark-green cloth for all other regiments, single-breasted (Illus. 1068).

Collar—the same color as the officer's coat, with tabs where appropriate, but without buttons. (Note: In the L.-Gds. Horse Regiment the collar and cuffs are red, while in all Cuirassier and Hussar regiments they are the color of the officer's undress coat.)

Cuffs—the same color as for officers, coming to a sharp point in front for Lancers and Hussars, without buttons.

Skirttails—cut away at a slant, of the same cloth as the coat. Flaps on the pockets for Dragoon and Hussar orderlies, as for general-officers' undress coats. In Jäger regiments flaps are not authorized.

Piping on collar and cuffs the same color as for officers, with the exception of red cuffs, for which piping is not authorized.

Buttons are covered with cloth the same color as the coat. *Lining* is the same color as the coat.

c.) *Pants*—dark-green cloth, with piping of the lining color of that unit to which the orderly belongs (Illus. 1068).

d.) *Riding trousers*—grey blue, with piping (Illus. 1068).

e.) *Chekmen coat*—in all respects similar to an officer's cossack *chekmen*, but without a girdle.

f.) *Sharavary pants*—as for officers.

g.) *Half-caftans* for orderlies with the troops of the Separate Caucasus Corps are in all respects the same as for officers, but without piping down the front or on the flaps, and with covered buttons.

h.) *Greatcoat*—of officer pattern, dark blue for Gendarmes, of grey cloth for all others. Standing collar the same color as for officers. Stripes on the cape the same color as the standing collar or colored tabs on it (if the standing collar is the same color as the greatcoat). The stripes are sewn on in three rows in the Guards and Military Educational institutions, and in two for all others. Buttons are struck in the same pattern as for officers.

i.) Helmets and fleece headdresses are as related in Order No. 121 of 31 October of this year (199).

28 December 1858 [sic - should be 1852 - M.C.] - To supplement the preceding description HIGHEST Authority orders that:

1.) In Cossack forces orderlies have officer pattern *shapka* headdresses, but without honor scrolls or pompons, and with only a plate of the pattern for soldiers, if one exists (Illus. 1069).

2.) In Cossack regiments where *papakha* fleece headdresses are prescribed, orderlies are to have such, of officer pattern but without honor scrolls, galloon, and piping.

3.) The leather helmets prescribed for orderlies in Cossack units on 31 October are withdrawn (200).

NOTES

(1) *Collection of Laws and Regulations*, 1826, Book I, pgs. 105 et seq., and information received from the War Ministry's Commissariat Department.

(2) *Collection of Laws and Regulations*, 1826, Book III, pg. 161.

(3) Ibid., 1827, Book I, pg. 3.

(4) Ibid., 1827, Book IV, pgs. 17 and 19.

(5) Ibid., 1829, Book II, pgs. 6 and 7.

(6) Ibid., Book IV, pg. 115.

(7) Ibid., 1830, Book IV, pg. 401.

(8) Ibid., 1831, Book II, pg. 39.

(9) Ibid., 1832, Book II, pg. 545.

(10) Ibid., 1836, Book III, pg. 213.

(11) Ibid., 1837, Book III, pg. 47.

(12) Ibid., Book IV, pg. 325.

(13) Order of the Minister of War, 23 January 1841, No. 8.

(14) Ditto, 18 April 1843, No. 51.

(15) Ditto, 2 January 1844, No 1.

(16) Ditto, 1 December 1844, No. 144.

(17) Ditto, 19 December 1844, No. 156.

(18) Ditto, 13 October 1849, No. 104.

(19) Ditto, 15 February 1850, No. 13.

(20) *Collection of Laws and Regulations*, 1826, Book I, pg. 103.

(21) Ibid., pgs. 105 et seq., and information received from the War Ministry's Commissariat Department.

(22) *Collection of Laws and Regulations*, 1826, Book III, pg. 161.

(23) Ibid., 1827, Book I, pg. 3.

(24) Ibid., Book IV, pgs. 17 and 19.

(25) Ibid., 1829, Book II, pg. 225.

(26) Ibid., pgs. 6 and 7.

(27) Ibid., Book IV, pg. 115.

(28) Ibid., 1830, Book IV, pg. 401.

(29) Ibid., 1831, Book II, pg. 39.

(30) Ibid., 1832, Book II, pg. 545.

(31) Ibid., 1836, Book II, pg. 213.

(32) Ibid., 1837, Book III, pg. 47.

(33) Ibid., Book IV, pg. 325.

(34) Order of the Minister of War, 23 January 1841, No. 8.

(35) Ditto, 18 April 1843, No. 51.

(36) Ditto, 2 January 1844, No. 1.

(37) Ditto, 1 December 1844, No. 144.

(38) Ditto, 19 December 1844, No. 156.

(39) Ditto, 13 October and 3 December 1849, Nos. 104 and 121.

(40) Ditto, 15 February 1850, No. 13.

(41) Ditto, 18 February 1854, No. 21.

(42) Ditto, 29 April 1854, No. 53.

(43) *Collection of Laws and Regulations*, 1826, Book I, pgs. 105 et seq.

(44) Ibid., Book III, pg. 161.

(45) Ibid., 1827, Book I, pg. 3.

(46) Ibid., Book IV, pgs. 17 and 19.

(47) Ibid., 1829, Book III, pgs. 6 and 7.

(48) Ibid., Book IV, pg. 115.

(49) Ibid., 1830, Book IV, pg 401.

(50) Ibid., 1832, Book II, pg. 545.

(51) Ibid., 1837, Book III, pg. 47.

(52) Ibid., Book IV, pg. 325.

(53) Order of the Minister of War, 23 January 1841, No. 8.

(54) Ditto, 18 April 1843, No. 51.

(55) Memorandum of the Duty General of HIS IMPERIAL MAJESTY'S Main Headquarters to the War Ministry's Commissariat, 29 December 1843, No. 12,551.

(56) Order of the Minister of War, 2 January 1844, No. 1.

(57) Ditto, 7 August 1849, No. 71.

(58) Ditto, 13 October and 3 December 1849, Nos. 104 and 121.

(59) Ditto, 15 February 1850, No. 13.

(60) *Collection of Laws and Regulations*, 1826, Book I, pgs. 105 et seq.

(61) Ibid., Book III, pg. 161.

(62) Ibid., 1827, Book 1, pg. 3.

(63) Ibid., Book IV, pgs. 17 and 19.

(64) Ibid., 1829, Book IV, pg. 115.

(65) Ibid., 1832, Book II, pg. 545.

(66) Ibid., 1837, Book III, pg. 47.

(67) Ibid., Book IV, pg. 325.

(68) Order of the Minister of War, 23 January 1841, No. 8.

(69. Ditto, 2 January 1844, No. 1.

(70) Ditto, 7 December 1844, No. 147, and information received from the War Ministry's Commissariat Department.

(71) Order of the Minister of War, 13 October and 3 December 1849, Nos. 104 and 121.

(72) Ditto, 15 February 1850, No. 13.

(73) Ditto, 29 April 1854, No. 53.

(74) *Collection of Laws and Regulations*, 1826, Book I, pgs. 105 et seq.

(75) Ibid., 1827, Book I, pg. 3.

(76) Ibid., Book IV, pgs. 17 and 19.

(77) Ibid., 1829, Book IV, pg. 115.

(78) Ibid., 1830, Book IV, pg. 401.

(79) Ibid., 1832, Book II, pg. 545.

(80) Ibid., 1837, Book III, pg. 47.

(81) Ibid., Book IV, pg. 325.

(82) Order of the Minister of War, 23 January 1841, No. 8.

(83) Ditto, 2 January 1844, No. 1.

(84) Ditto, 7 December 1844, No. 147, and information received from the War Ministry's Commissariat Department.

(85) *Collection of Laws and Regulations*, 1826, Book I, pgs. 105 et seq., and information received from the War Ministry's Commissariat Department.

(86) *Collection of Laws and Regulations*, 1826, Book III, pg. 161.

(87) Ibid., 1827, Book I, pg. 3.

(88) Ibid., Book IV, pgs. 17 and 19.

(89) Ibid., 1829, Book II, pg. 6.

(90) Ibid., Book IV, pgs. 115 and 116.

(91) Ibid., 1830, Book IV, pg. 401.

(92) Ibid., 1832, Book II, pg. 545.

(93) Ibid., 1837, Book III, pg. 47.

(94) Ibid., Book IV, pg. 325.

(95) Order of the Minister of War, 23 January 1841, No. 8.

(96) Ditto, 2 January 1844, No. 1.

(97) Ditto, 30 April 1846, No. 75.

(98) Memorandum of the Minister of War to Lieutenant-General Prince Dolgorukov, 4 November 1846, No. 10,112.

(99) Order of the Minister of War, 20 June 1849, No. 57.

(100) Ditto, 13 October and 3 December 1849, Nos. 104 and 121.

(101) Ditto, 20 October 1849, No. 106.

(102) Ditto, 31 October 1849, No. 108.

(103) Ditto, 22 December 1849, No. 132.

(104) Ditto, 15 February 1850, No. 13.

(105) Memorandum of the Minister of War to the Minister of Internal Affairs, 19 April 1850, No. 3526.

(106) Order of the Minister of War, 30 November 1850, No. 82.

(107) *Description of the Uniforms and Weapons of officers of the forces of the IMPERIAL Russian Army in 1845*, Book III, pg. 42; directive from the War Ministry's Inspection Department to the Military Campaign Stable Master of HIS IMPERIAL MAJESTY'S Main Headquarters, Lieutenant-Colonel Beklemishev, 2 August 1836, No. 6252, and information received from the Military Campaign Stable Master of HIS IMPERIAL MAJESTY'S Main Headquarters.

(108) Order of the Minister of War, 2 January 1844, No. 1, and information received from the Military Campaign Stable Master of HIS IMPERIAL MAJESTY'S Main Headquarters.

(109) Order of the Ministery of War, 7 December 1844, No. 144, and supplementary information received from the War Ministry's Commissariat Department.

(110) Order of the Minister of War, 4 January 1845, No. 1.

(111) Information received from the Commander of the Feldjäger Corps.

(112) HIGHEST Confirmed description of uniforms for the Feldjäger Corps, 26 May 1826, in the files of the Inspection Department of

HIS IMPERIAL MAJESTY'S Main Headquarters, 1826, No. 156.

(113) *Collection of Laws and Regulations Relating to the Military Administration*, 1832, Book II, pg. 545.

(114) Order of the Minister of War, 2 January 1844, No. 1.

(115) Ditto, 14 March 1845, No. 44.

(116) Ditto, 13 October 1849, No. 104.

(117) *Complete Collection of Laws of the Russian Empire* [*Polnoe Sobranie Zakonov*, henceforth PSZ], Second collection, Vol. I, No. 141, pg. 200, § 4.

(118) Ibid., No. 171, pg. 242.

(119) *Collection of Laws and Regulations*, 1834, Book I, pgs. 529-539, and *Description of the Uniforms and Weapons of officers of the forces of the IMPERIAL Russian Army in 1845*, Book III, pg. 304.

(120) *Collection of Laws and Regulations*, 1834, Book II, pg. 231.

(121) Ibid., pg. 175.

(122) Ibid., pg. 283.

(123) Ibid., 1836, Book III, pgs. 731 et seq.

(124) Ibid., 1837, Book III, pg. 47.

(125) Ibid., Book IV, pg. 325.

(126) Order of the Minister of War, 2 January 1844, No. 1.

(127) Ditto, 20 July 1849, No. 57.

(128) Ditto, 27 September 1849, No. 97.

(129) 13 October and 3 December 1849, Nos. 104 and 121.

(130) PSZ, Second Collection, Vol. I, No. 141, pg. 200, § 3.

(131) Ibid., No. 171, pg. 242.

(132) Ibid., No. 491, pg. 808, and *Description of the Uniforms and Weapons of officers of the forces of the IMPERIAL Russian Army in 1845*, Book III, pg. 307, § 5.

(133) *Description of the Uniforms and Weapons of officers of the forces of the IMPERIAL Russian Army in 1845*, Book III, pgs. 305-308, and information received from the War Ministry's Commissariat Department.

(134) Memorandum of the Minister of War to the Commander-in-Chief of the Separate Caucasus Corps, 4 July 1850, No. 5016.

(135) Order of the Minister of War, 2 February 1852, No. 17.

(136) Ditto, 2 March 1852, No. 28.

(137) Ditto, 28 May 1852, No. 59.

(138) Ditto, 29 April 1854, No. 53, and information received from the War Ministry's Commissariat Department.

(139) Memorandum of the Minister of War to the Commander-in-Chief of the Separate Caucasus Corps, 1 May 1854, No. 4950.

(140) Order of the Minister of War, 11 October 1854, No. 106.

(141) *Description of the Uniforms and Weapons of officers of the forces of the IMPERIAL Russian Army in 1845*, Book III, pg. 309.

(142) Ibid., pgs. 309-311.

(143) PSZ, Second Collection, Vol. I, No. 141, pg. 200, § 3.

(144) Ibid., No. 491, pg. 808, and *Description of the Uniforms and Weapons of officers of the forces of the IMPERIAL Russian Army in 1845*, Book III, pg. 307, § 5.

(145) *Description of the Uniforms and Weapons of officers of the forces of the IMPERIAL Russian Army in 1845*, Book III, pg. 313, and information received from the War Ministry's Commissariat Department.

(146) Order of the Minister of War, 2 February 1852, No. 17.

(147) Ditto, 29 April 1854, No. 53.

(148) *Description of the Uniforms and Weapons of officers of the forces of the IMPERIAL Russian Army in 1845*, Book III, pgs. 313-314.

(149) Order of the Minister of War, 2 February 1852, No. 17.

(150) *Description of the Uniforms and Weapons of officers of the forces of the IMPERIAL Russian Army in 1845*, Book III, pg. 314, and information received from the War Ministry's Commissariat Department.

(151) Order of the Minister of War, 27 November 1850, No. 81.

(152) Memorandum of the Minister of War to HIS IMPERIAL HIGHNESS Commanding the Guards and Grenadier Corps, 17 March 1851, No. 2597.

(153) Order of the Minister of War, 2 February 1852, No. 17.

(154) Ditto, 29 April 1854, No. 53.

(155) *Description of the Uniforms and Weapons of officers of the forces of the IMPERIAL Russian Army in 1845*, Book III, pgs. 314-317, information received from the War Ministry's Commissariat Department, and *Collection of Laws and Regulations Regarding the Military Administration*, 1836, Book III, pgs. 731-737, § 16.

(156) Order of the Minister of War, 2 February 1852, No. 17.

(157) PSZ, Second Collection, Vol. 1, No. 141, pg. 200, § 3.

(158) Order of the Minister of War, 2 February 1852, No. 17.

(159) File of the former Orderly Room of the Chief Director of the Corps of Pages and Cadet Corps, 1827, No. 328/22, preserved in the Archive of the Headquarters of HIS IMPERIAL HIGHNESS the Chief Commander of Military Educational Institutions.

(160) *Collection of Laws and Regulations Relating to the Military Administration*, 1836, Book III, pg. 701, §§ 68, 69, and 70, and *Description of the Uniforms and Weapons of officers of the forces of the IMPERIAL Russian Army in 1845*, Book III, pgs. 302-304.

(161) Order of the Chief Commander of the Corps of Pages, all Army Cadet Corps, and the Nobiliary Regiment, 20 December 1840, No. 306.

(162) HIGHEST Confirmed directive on the reorganization of the St.-Petersburg Military Orphans Section, 26 November 1826, § 31, and statements from persons who were at this time in the St.-Petersburg Battalion of Military Cantonists .

(163) HIGHEST Order to the acting chief of the War Ministry from the chief of HIS IMPERIAL MAJESTY'S Main Headquarters, 19 November 1831, No. 470, and information received from the War Ministry's Commissariat Department.

(164) Information received from the War Ministry's Commissariat Department.

(165) HIGHEST Order from the Duty General of HIS IMPERIAL MAJESTY'S Main Headquarters to the Military Educational Administration for Military Cantonists, 10 July 1835, No. 83.

(166) HIGHEST Confirmed directive on the reorganization of the Voronezh Battalion of Military Cantonists, 8 November 1836, § 21.

(167) Information received in the St.-Petersburg Battalion of Military Cantonists.

(168) Order of the Minister of War, 19 May 1847, No. 86.

(169) Memorandum of the Duty General of HIS IMPERIAL MAJESTY'S Main Headquarters to the Department of Military Settlements, 22 June 1848, No. 5889.

(170) Order of the Minister of War, 10 January 1852, No. 4, § 45.

(171) PSZ, Second Collection, Vol. II, No. 1366, pg. 775, § 5.

(172) Ibid., No. 5253, pg. 167, § 6.

(173) Regulation on the War Ministry's Auditors School, 11 September 1846.

(174) HIGHEST Order to the Department of Military Settlements, 8 November 1854, No. 730.

(175) *Collection of Laws and Regulations Relating to the Military Administration*, 1835, Book I, pg. 639, § 11.

(176) HIGHEST Confirmed Regulation on forming Cavalry squadrons and Artillery batteries from military cantonists in Cavalry Military Settlement Districts , 8 August 1836, § 23.

(177) Information received from the War Ministry's Commissariat Department.

(178) Order of the Minister of War, 19 May 1847, No. 86.

(179) Information received from the War Ministry's Commissariat Department.

(180) PSZ, Second Collection, Vol. VI, Sect. I, No. 4495, pg. 298 § 7, and information received in Military Educational Institutions.

(181) Order of the Minister of War, 14 July 1853, No. 54.

(182) *Description of the Uniforms and Weapons of officers of the forces of the IMPERIAL Russian Army in 1845*, Book III, pg. 293.

(183) PSZ, Second Collection, Vol. I, No. 141, pg. 201, and information received from the War Ministry's Commissariat Department.

(184) Information received from this same department.

(185) Order of the Minister of War, 5 May 1844, No. 60, and information received in the Headquarters of Military Educational Institutions.

(186) Order of the Minister of War, 21 January 1846, No. 18.

(187) Ditto, 15 March 1846, No. 50.

(188) Ditto, 19 May 1847, No. 86.

(189) Ditto, 2 December 1849, No. 123.

(190) Information received in the War Ministry's Commissariat Department, and HIGHEST Confirmed organizational tables for Military Educational Institutions.

(191) *Collection of Laws and Regulations Relating to the Military Administration*, 1835, Book III, pg. 213, and information received from the War Ministry's Commissariat Department.

(192) Information received from the War Ministry's Commissariat Department.

(193) Order of the Minister of War, 19 May 1847, No. 86, and an order of the Main Chief of Military Educational Institutions, 7 July 1847, No. 874.

(194) Memorandum of the Minister of War to the Main Chief of Military Educational Institutions, 21 May 1853, No. 6421, and an order of the Main Chief of Military Educational Institutions, 8 July 1853, No. 1748.

(195) *Description of the Uniforms and Weapons of officers of the forces of the IMPERIAL Russian Army in 1845*, Book III, pg. 292.

(196) PSZ, Second Collection, Vol. I, No. 141, pg. 201.

(197) Order of the Minister of War, 3 October 1848, No. 168.

(198) Ditto, 31 October 1852, No. 121.

(199) Ditto, 28 December 1852, No. 148.

(200) The same order.

РИСУНКИ

ОДЕЖДЫ и ВООРУЖЕНІЯ

РОССІЙСКИХЪ

ВОЙСКЪ

1825-1855·

PLATES LIST OF ILLUSTRATIONS

1024. Staff-Doctor in the Guards forces, 1852-1854.

1025. Helmet plate for Students of the St.-Petersburg Medical-Surgical Academy, established 28 May 1852.

1026. Shoulder straps on Military Doctors' campaign greatcoats, established 29 April 1854.

1027. Field and Coy-Grade Officers' shoulder straps for dress coats and frock coats of Military Doctors, 11 October 1854.

1028. Senior and Junior Veterinary Doctors, 1826-1852.

1029. Quartermaster. Guards Corps, 1826-1852.

1030. Riding Master. 1826-1850.

1031. Riding Masters. Riding Masters School, 1826-1850.

1032. Chief Riding Master. Guards Riding Master School, 1850-1851.

1033. Coat collar embroidery for the Chief Riding Master of the Guards Riding Master School, established 27 November 1850.

1034. Coat cuff and cuff-flap embroidery for the Chief Riding Master of the Guards Riding Master School, 27 Nov.1850.

1035. Coat collar and cuff embroidery for Senior Riding Masters of the Guards Riding Master School, November 1850.

1036. Coat collar and cuff embroidery for Junior Riding Masters of the Guards Riding Master School, November 1850.

1037. Student. Guards Riding Master School, 1850-51.

1038. Senior and Junior Riding Masters. Guards Riding Master School, 1851-1855.

1039. Shoulder strap for Students at the Guards Riding Master School, established 17 March 1851.

1040. Guards and Army Bandmasters. 1826-1852.

1041. Arsenal Inspector [*Tseikhvarter*]. 1826-1852.

1042. Coat collar and cuff embroidery for Professors at Military Educational Institutions, established in 1827.

1043. Professor and Instructor. Military Educational Institutions, 1827-1836.

1044. Coat collar embroidery for Civilian Officials on the Instructional Staff of Military Edu. Institutions, 27 May 1836.

1045. Coat cuff embroidery for Civilian Officials on the Instructional Staff of Mil. Educational Institutions, 27 May 1836.

1046. Class Inspector and Science Instructor. Military Educational Institutions, 1836-1840.

1047. Class Inspector and Teacher-Examiner [*Nastavnik-Nablyudatel'*]. Military Educational Institutions, 1840-1855.

1048. Science Instructor and Tutor. Military Educational Institutions 1840-1855.

1049. Assistant Fencing Instructor. Military Educational Institutions, 1840-1855

1050. Cantonist. 1st Company of the St.-Petersburg Battalion of Military Cantonists, 1826-1831.

1051. Cantonists. 2nd and 3rd Companies of the St.-Petersburg Battalion of Military Cantonists, 1826-1831.

1052. Cantonist. 4th and 5th Companies of the St.-Petersburg Battalion of Military Cantonists,1826-1831.

1053. Cantonist. Battalions, Half-Battalions, and Separate Companies of Military Cantonists, 1831-1855.

1054. Instructor of NCO Rank. Battalions, Half-Battalions, and Separate Companies of Military Cantonists, 1831-1845.

1055. Instructor of Non-Commissioned Officer Rank. St.-Petersburg Battalion of Military Cantonists, 1845-1855.

1056. Student. Auditors School at the St.-Petersburg Battalion of Military Cantonists, 1832-1855.

1057. Pupil. Young Noble Boys Section of the Novgorod Battalion of Military Cantonists, 1834-1844.

1058. Cantonists. Cavalry squadrons and Artillery batteries in districts of Cavalry Military Settlements, 1836-1855. *1. Army Cuirassier regiments, 2. Lancer and Hussar regiments, and 3. Horse-Artillery batteries.*

1059. Cantonists. L.-Gds. Semenovskii and His Majesty's Cavalier Guards Regiments, 1832-1855 .

1060. Cantonist. Military Educational Institutions, 1831-1855. (*1st Cadet Corps.*)

1061. Clerk in the War Ministry, 1826-1844. Hospital Orderly [*Fel'dsher*] in Military Hospitals, 1826-1855.

1062. Shoulder straps for Clerks in the War Ministry and its subordinate offices, established in 1844. *a) General Staff Department; b) Inspection and Engineer Departments; c) Artillery and Auditors Departments; d) Commissariat Department; e) Provisioning Department; f) Military Settlements Department; g) Medical Department; h) War Ministry Chancellery; i) Military Academic Commmittee; j.) Committee Established 13 August 1814; l) Military Stud Farms; m) and n) Military Educational Institutions.*

1063. Keeper. Provisioning Administration, 1846-1855.

1064. Lower ranks' shoulder straps in the Headquarters of the Inspector of All Art. and of the Inspector for Eng., 1849.

1065. Clerk. Military Educational Institutions, 1826-1855. (*2nd Cadet Corps.*) 1066. Private from the Guards forces. Service Companies at Military Educational Institutions, 1826-1855. (*Paul Cadet Corps.*)

1067. Adjutant's Orderly, 1826-1852.

1068. Orderlies. Guards Cavalry and Army Infantry, 1852-1855.

1069. Orderly. Guards Cossack units, 1852-1855.

Army Infantry Staff Duty Officer, 1826-1844

Staff Duty Officer. Separate Corps of the Internal Guard, 1826-1844

Guards Infantry Staff Duty Officer, 1826-1844

Army Infantry Staff Duty Officer, 1844-1855

Infantry Staff Duty Officer. Separate Caucasus Corps, 1850-1855

Guards Adjutants. Infantry, 1826-1844, and Cavalry. 1826-1830.

Army Cavalry Adjutant, 1829-1844

Guards Cavalry Adjutant, 1844-1855

Adjutant. Separate Corps of the Internal Guard, 1844-1855

Army Infantry Town Commandant, 1826-1844. Guards Cavalry Town Commandant, 1826-1830

Guards Infantry Town Adjutant, 1826-1844

Army Infantry Town Adjutant, 1849-1855

Guards Infantry Provost [Geval diger], 1826-1844

Army Infantry Provost, 1826-1844

Army Wagon Master, 1826-1830

Guards Senior Wagon Master. 1844-1855

Field-Grade Officer at large in the Army, 1826-1849

Company-Grade Officer at large in the Cavalry, 1826-1829

Company-Grade Officer at large in the Army, 1826-1849

Company-Grade Officers at large in the Army and in the Cavalry, 1849-1855

Police Commandants [Politsiimeistery] in the capitals and in provincial cities, 1849-1855

Military Campaign Stable Master. HIS IMPERIAL MAJESTY'S Main Headquarters, 1836-1844

Military Campaign Stable Master. HIS IMPERIAL MAJESTY'S Main Headquarters, 1844-1855

Feldjäger and Company-Grade Officer. Feldjäger Corps, 1826-1845

Feldjäger. 1826-1855

Company-Grade Officers of the Feldjäger Corps, and Feldjäger, 1845-1855

Officer's helmet plate for the Feldjäger Corps, authorized 14 March 1845

Shoulder strap for Civilian Officials of the War Ministry, 1st and 2nd Categories, established 4 March 1834

Civilian Officials. HIS IMPERIAL MAJESTY'S Main Headquarters, 1st and 2nd Categories, 1826-1834

Civilian Officials. Ministry of War, 3rd and 4th Categories, 1826-1834

Civilian Official. Military Topography Depot of HIS IMPERIAL MAJESTY'S Main Headquarters, 3rd Category, 1826-1834

1007

Field-Grade Officer and Company-Grade Officer. Ministry of War, 1834-1849. From the Light Cavalry and Infantry

Company-Grade Officers. Ministry of War, 1834-1849. From the Infantry and Heavy Cavalry

Civilian Officials. Ministry of War, 1st and 2nd Categories, 1834-1855

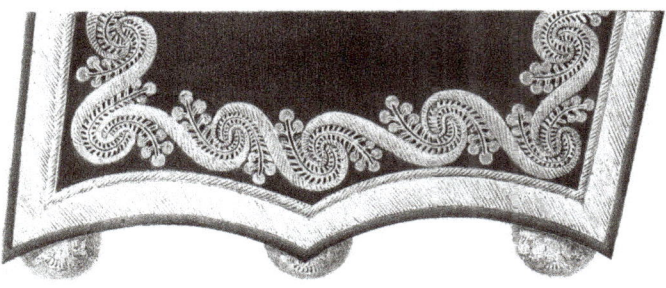

Coat collar embroidery for Civilian Officials in the War Ministry, 1st Category, established 4 March 1834

Coat cuff, cuff-flap, and pocket-flap embroidery for Civilian Officials of the War Ministry, 1st Category, established 4 March 1834

Civilian Officials. Ministry of War, 3rd and 4th Categories, 1834-1855

Civilian Official. Ministry of War, 5th Category, 1834-1855

Civilian Officials. Ministry of War, 1st Category, 1834-1855

Civilian Officials. Ministry of War, all Categories (in greatcoat), and 2nd, 3rd, 4th, and 5th Categories (in undress uniform), 1834-1855

Civilian Officials. Offices subordinate to the Ministry of War, 1st and 2nd Categories, 1834-1855

Civilian Officials. Offices subordinate to the Ministry of War, 3rd and 4th Categories, 1834-1855

Infantry Company-Grade Officer. Offices subordinate to the Ministry of War, 1834-1849

Shabrack, pistol holder, and saddle for Generals and Field and Company-Grade Officers of the War Ministry, for whom this organization's uniform is prescribed, established 19 June 1854

Helmet plate for Students of the St.-Petersburg Medical-Surgical Academy, established 28 May 1852

Infantry Field-Grade Officer. Offices subordinate to the Ministry of War, 1849-1855

Chief Inspector of the Army Medical Administration and Field Staff-Doctor General, 1826-1852

Staff-Doctor and Doctor, 1826-1852

Staff-Doctor in the Guards forces 1852-1854

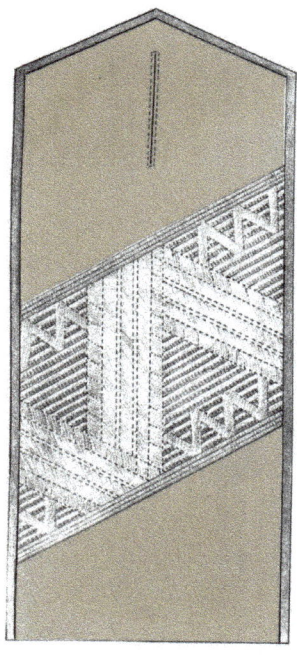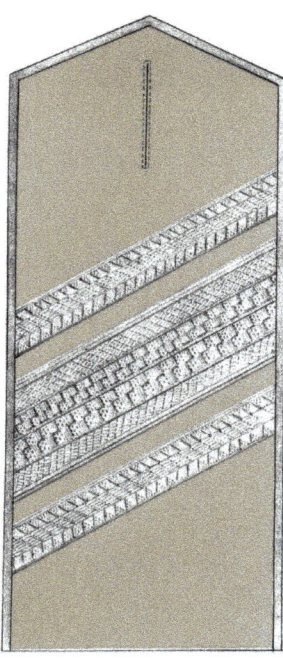

Shoulder straps on Military Doctors' campaign greatcoats, established 29 April 1854

Field and Company-Grade Officers' shoulder straps for dress coats and frock coats of Military Doctors, established 11 October 1854

Senior and Junior Veterinary Doctors, 1826-1852

Quartermaster. Guards Corps, 1826-1852

Riding Master. 1826-1850.

Riding Masters. Riding Masters School, 1826-1850

Chief Riding Master. Guards Riding Master School, 1850-1851

Coat collar embroidery for the Chief Riding Master of the Guards Riding Master School, established 27 November 1850

Coat cuff and cuff-flap embroidery for the Chief Riding Master of the Guards Riding Master School, established 27 November 1850

Coat collar and cuff embroidery for Senior Riding Masters of the Guards Riding Master School, established 27 November 1850
Coat collar and cuff embroidery for Junior Riding Masters of the Guards Riding Master School, established 27 November 1850

Student. Guards Riding Master School, 1850-51

Senior and Junior Riding Masters. Guards Riding Master School, 1851-1855

Shoulder strap for Students at the Guards Riding Master School, established 17 March 1851

Coat collar and cuff embroidery for Professors at Military Educational Institutions, established in 1827

Guards and Army Bandmasters. 1826-1852

Arsenal Inspector [Tseikhvarter]. 1826-1852

Professor and Instructor. Military Educational Institutions, 1827-1836

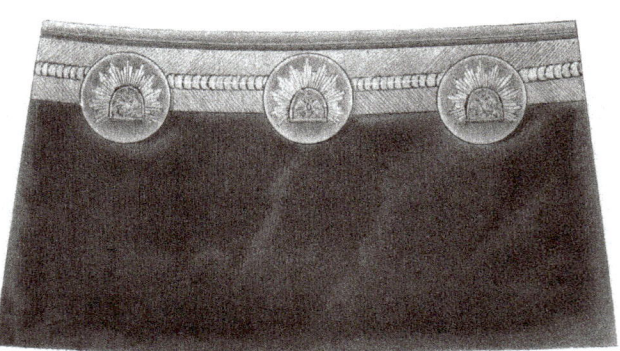

Coat collar embroidery for Civilian Officials on the Instructional Staff of Military Educational Institutions, established 27 May 1836

Class Inspector and Science Instructor. Military Educational Institutions, 1836-1840

Class Inspector and Teacher-Examiner [Nastavnik-Nablyudatel]. Military Educational Institutions, 1840-1855

Science Instructor and Tutor. Military Educational Institutions, 1840-1855

Assistant Fencing Instructor. Military Educational Institutions, 1840-1855

Cantonist. 1st Company of the St.-Petersburg Battalion of Military Cantonists, 1826-1831

1051

Cantonists. 2nd and 3rd Companies of the St.-Petersburg Battalion of Military Cantonists, 1826-1831

Cantonist. 4th and 5th Companies of the St.-Petersburg Battalion of Military Cantonists,1826-1831

Cantonist. Battalions, Half-Battalions, and Separate Companies of Military Cantonists, 1831-1855

Instructor of Non-Commissioned Officer Rank. Battalions, Half-Battalions, and Separate Companies of Military Cantonists, 1831-1845

Instructor of Non-Commissioned Officer Rank. St.-Petersburg Battalion of Military Cantonists, 1845-1855

Student. Auditors School at the St.-Petersburg Battalion of Military Cantonists, 1832-1855

Pupil. Young Noble Boys Section of the Novgorod Battalion of Military Cantonists, 1834-1844

Cantonists. Cavalry squadrons and Artillery batteries in districts of Cavalry Military Settlements, 1836-1855.
1. Army Cuirassier regiments, 2. Lancer and Hussar regiments, and 3. Horse-Artillery batteries

Cantonists. L.-Gds. Semenovskii and His Majesty's Cavalier Guards Regiments, 1832-1855

Cantonist. Military Educational Institutions, 1831-1855. (1st Cadet Corps.) Note: Until 1835 shoulder straps and forage-cap bands were without numbers and letters

Clerk in the War Ministry, 1826-1844. Hospital Orderly [Feldsher] in Military Hospitals, 1826-1855

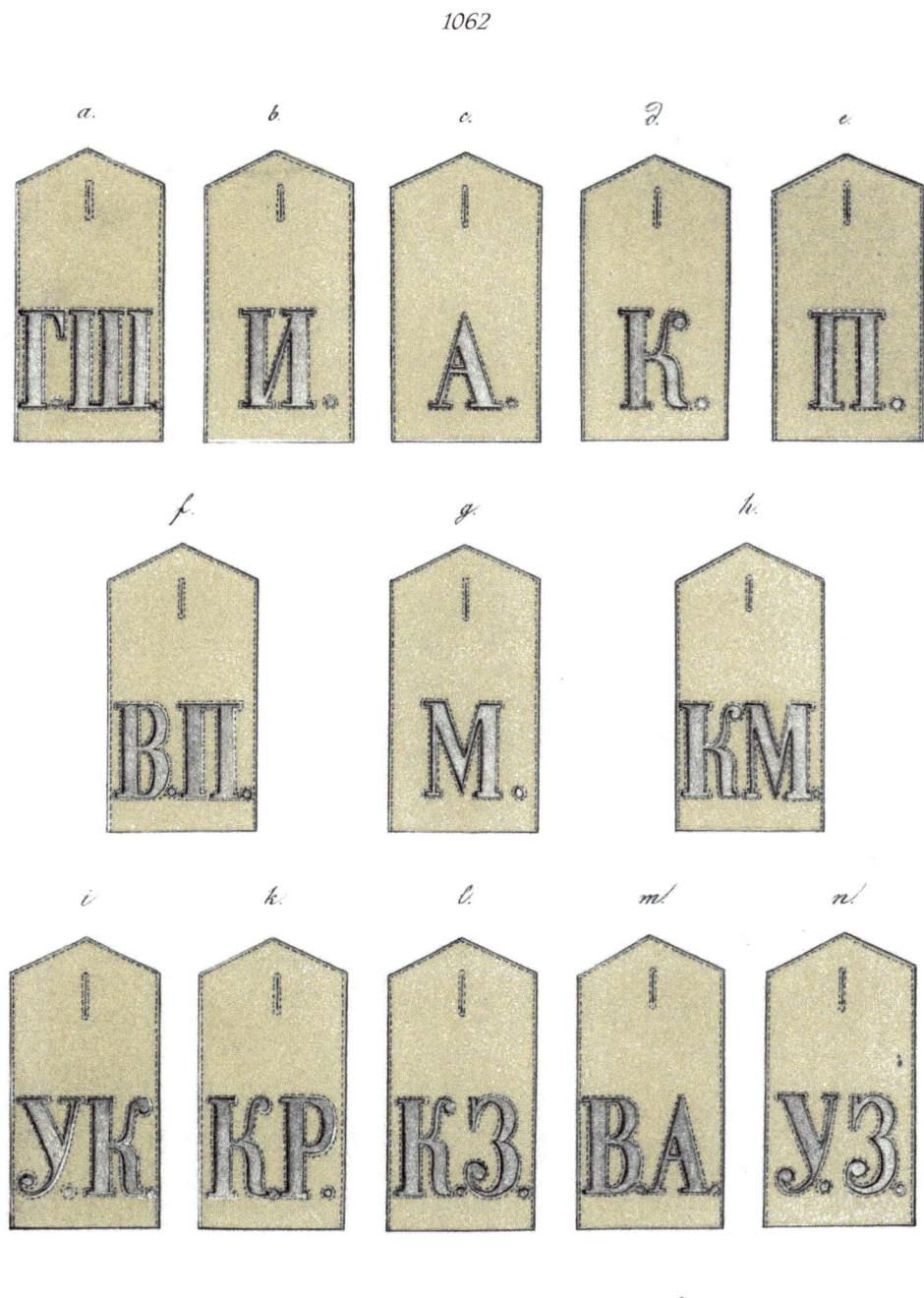

Shoulder straps for Clerks in the War Ministry and its subordinate offices, established in 1844. *a*) General Staff Department; *b*) Inspection and Engineer Departments; *c*) Artillery and Auditors Departments; *d*) Commissariat Department; *e*) Provisioning Department; *f*) Military Settlements Department; *g*) Medical Department; *h*) War Ministry Chancellery; *i*) Military Academic Committee; *j*) Committee Established 13 August 1814; *l*) Military Stud Farms; *m*) and *n*) Military Educational Institutions

1063

Keeper. Provisioning Administration, 1846-1855

Lower ranks' shoulder straps in the Headquarters of the Inspector of All Artillery and of the Inspector for Engineering, established 2 December 1849

Clerk. Military Educational Institutions, 1826-1855.
(2nd Cadet Corps.) Note: Until 1835 shoulder straps and forage-cap bands were without numbers and letters

Private from the Guards forces. Service Companies at Military Educational Institutions, 1826-1855. (Paul Cadet Corps.)

Adjutant's Orderly, 1826-1852

Orderlies. Guards Cavalry and Army Infantry, 1852-1855

Orderly. Guards Cossack units, 1852-1855

SOLDIERS, WEAPONS & UNIFORMS ALREADY PUBLISHED
(SOME TITLES)

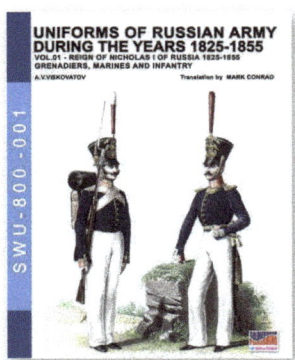

UNIFORMS OF RUSSIAN ARMY DURING THE YEARS 1825-1855
VOL.01 - REIGN OF NICHOLAS I OF RUSSIA 1825-1855
GRENADIERS, MARINES AND INFANTRY
A.V.VISKOVATOV — Translation by MARK CONRAD
SWU-800-001

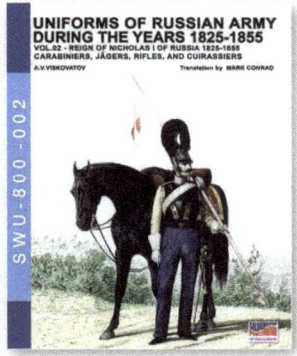

UNIFORMS OF RUSSIAN ARMY DURING THE YEARS 1825-1855
VOL.02 - REIGN OF NICHOLAS I OF RUSSIA 1825-1855
CARABINIERS, JÄGERS, RIFLES, AND CUIRASSIERS
A.V.VISKOVATOV — Translation by MARK CONRAD
SWU-800-002

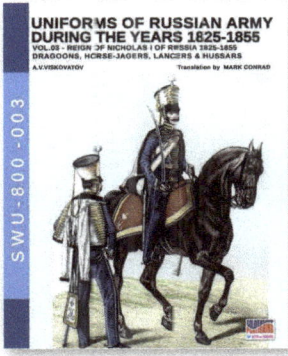

UNIFORMS OF RUSSIAN ARMY DURING THE YEARS 1825-1855
VOL.03 - REIGN OF NICHOLAS I OF RUSSIA 1825-1855
DRAGOONS, HORSE-JAGERS, LANCERS AND HUSSARS
A.V.VISKOVATOV — Translation by MARK CONRAD
SWU-800-003

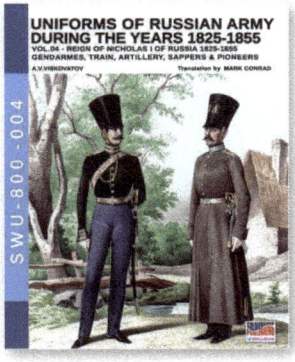

UNIFORMS OF RUSSIAN ARMY DURING THE YEARS 1825-1855
VOL.04 - REIGN OF NICHOLAS I OF RUSSIA 1825-1855
GENDARMES, TRAIN, ARTILLERY, SAPPERS & PIONEERS
A.V.VISKOVATOV — Translation by MARK CONRAD
SWU-800-004

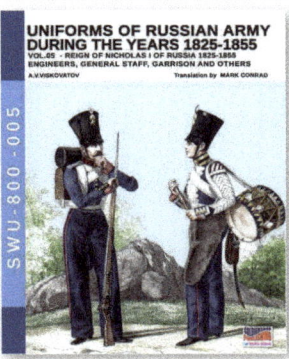

UNIFORMS OF RUSSIAN ARMY DURING THE YEARS 1825-1855
VOL.05 - REIGN OF NICHOLAS I OF RUSSIA 1825-1855
ENGINEERS, GENERAL STAFF, GARRISON AND OTHERS
A.V.VISKOVATOV — Translation by MARK CONRAD
SWU-800-005

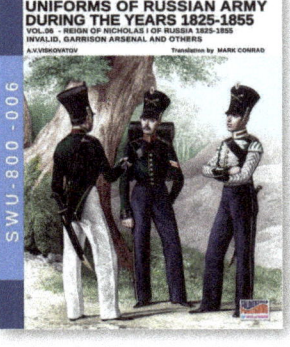

UNIFORMS OF RUSSIAN ARMY DURING THE YEARS 1825-1855
VOL.06 - REIGN OF NICHOLAS I OF RUSSIA 1825-1855
INVALID, GARRISON ARSENAL AND OTHERS
A.V.VISKOVATOV — Translation by MARK CONRAD
SWU-800-006

UNIFORMS OF RUSSIAN ARMY DURING THE YEARS 1825-1855
VOL.07 - REIGN OF NICHOLAS I OF RUSSIA 1825-1855
GUARDS INFANTRY & GUARDS CUIRASSIERS REGIMENTS
A.V.VISKOVATOV — Translation by MARK CONRAD
SWU-800-007

IMPERIAL SOLDIERS & UNIFORMS 1640-1860
IN THE ART OF FRANZ GERASCH
LUCA S.CRISTINI — Plates by FRANZ GERASCH
SWU-GEN-001

UNIFORMS OF EUROPEAN ARMIES DURING THE BATAVIAN REVOLUTION
FROM THE AMSTERDAM CIVIC GUARD TO FOREIGN ARMIES: FRENCH, DUTCH, ENGLISH, AUSTRIAN, PRUSSIAN AND GERMAN STATESIN THE YEARS 1790-1797
LUCA STEFANO CRISTINI — J.D.LANGENDIJK — S.D.CASTEN
SWU-NAP-001

POLISH SOLDIERS DURING THE NAPOLEONIC WARS
THE POLISH LEGIONS, THE ARMY OF THE DUCHY OF WARSAW AND THE POLISH IN THE GRAND ARMÉE
LUCA STEFANO CRISTINI
SWU-NAP-002

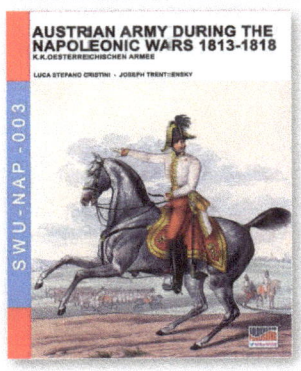

AUSTRIAN ARMY DURING THE NAPOLEONIC WARS 1813-1818
K.K.OESTERREICHISCHEN ARMEE
LUCA STEFANO CRISTINI — JOSEPH TRENTSENSKY
SWU-NAP-003

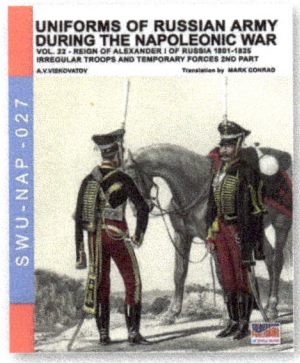

UNIFORMS OF RUSSIAN ARMY DURING THE NAPOLEONIC WAR
VOL. 22 - REIGN OF ALEXANDER I OF RUSSIA 1801-1825
IRREGULAR TROOPS AND TEMPORARY FORCES 2ND PART
A.V.VISKOVATOV — Translation by MARK CONRAD
SWU-NAP-027

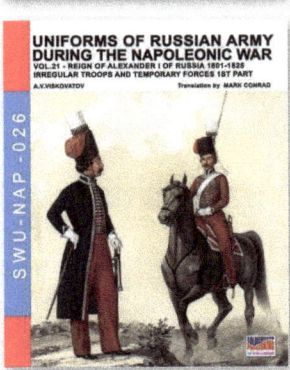

UNIFORMS OF RUSSIAN ARMY DURING THE NAPOLEONIC WAR
VOL.21 - REIGN OF ALEXANDER I OF RUSSIA 1801-1825
IRREGULAR TROOPS AND TEMPORARY FORCES 1ST PART
A.V.VISKOVATOV — Translation by MARK CONRAD
SWU-NAP-026

UNIFORMS OF RUSSIAN ARMY DURING THE NAPOLEONIC WAR
VOL.20 - REIGN OF ALEXANDER I OF RUSSIA 1801-1825
MILITARY EDUCATIONAL INSTITUTIONS, FLAGS & STANDARDS
A.V.VISKOVATOV — Translation by MARK CONRAD
SWU-NAP-025

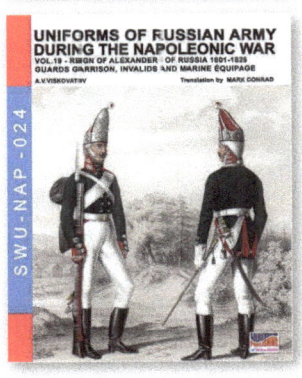

UNIFORMS OF RUSSIAN ARMY DURING THE NAPOLEONIC WAR
VOL.19 - REIGN OF ALEXANDER I OF RUSSIA 1801-1825
GUARDS GARRISON, INVALIDS AND MARINE EQUIPAGE
A.V.VISKOVATOV — Translation by MARK CONRAD
SWU-NAP-024

UNIFORMS OF RUSSIAN ARMY DURING THE NAPOLEONIC WAR
VOL.18 - REIGN OF ALEXANDER I OF RUSSIA 1801-1825
GUARDS ARTILLERY, ENGINEERS & GENERAL STAFF
A.V.VISKOVATOV — Translation by MARK CONRAD
SWU-NAP-023

www.ingramcontent.com/pod-product-compliance
Lightning Source LLC
Chambersburg PA
CBHW041145120626
46547CB00020B/3110